To Judy,

JACKSON'S KENYA

A PEACE CORPS STORY

Richard Otto Wiegand

Library of Congress Cataloging-in-Publication Control Number: 2020920988

ISBN: 978-1-7348450-2-0

Cover and interior design: Debbi Stocco
Cover photo caption: Otto Wiegand, Jackson Sikolia, George Roemer – north of Kisumu – 2013

TABLE OF CONTENTS

Prologue 7

PART I—WELCOME TO THE PEACE CORPS

Chapter 1—Dreaming of the Nile..10
Chapter 2—How About Going to Kenya? 12
Chapter 3—Undoing the Ugly American 15
Chapter 4—Corps Values...17
Chapter 5—The Philadelphia Story 21
Chapter 6—Coastal Learning 23
Chapter 7—Lingua Franca...29
Chapter 8—Crossing the Equator 33
Chapter 9—Reminders of Destruction.......................................36

PART II—BETTINGTON

Chapter 10—Who Are You? 40
Chapter 11—Culinary Chronicles...42
Chapter 12—Too Much of a Good Thing....................................44
Chapter 13—Jambo Jackson..47
Chapter 14—Pictures and Popcorn 51
Chapter 15—The Good, The Bad, and The Colonials.................53
Chapter 16—Fare or Fowl? 60
Chapter 17—Up to Bats..63
Chapter 18—More Than A Paper Cut..65
Chapter 19—Colleague Potpourri..67
Chapter 20—Promise and Tragedy in Luo Land 72
Chapter 21—Defining Differences, Seeking Similarities 77
Chapter 22—Adventures on The Road.......................................82
Chapter 23—Broad Spectrum News...89
Chapter 24—Big Daddy, Big Problems......................................91
Chapter 25—Everyone Is Doing It 95
Chapter 26—Garnering a World View..98

Chapter 27—Home on The Scheme 103
Chapter 28—Rhythms in Time 106
Chapter 29—Honey of a Situation...108
Chapter 30—Fading Glory 110
Chapter 31—A Colonial Character..113
Chapter 32—Marriage Kenyan Style..115

PART III—ON THE JOB

Chapter 33—Discovering What's Out There...............................118
Chapter 34—Better Rumination 127
Chapter 35—Minimizing the Bull 130
Chapter 36—Immersion for Life 133
Chapter 37—Showing Their Stuff 135
Chapter 38—Promoting Chacha..137
Chapter 39—Cooperating Kenyan Style 139
Chapter 40—Cash Cow 161
Chapter 41—Firing the Milkman...164
Chapter 42—Big City West 166
Chapter 43—My Town 170

PART IV—NAIROBI

Chapter 44—Where Cultures Collide..174
Chapter 45—Out of Africa and Back Again 178
Chapter 46—Country Cool 180
Chapter 47—Thumbing Around 182
Chapter 48—See You at Your Site 186

PART V—TONGAREN

Chapter 49—Going Native 190
Chapter 50—Snakes on The Plain 196
Chapter 51—Chewing Up the Place 199
Chapter 52—Becoming One with The People..............................201
Chapter 53—Scholarly Efforts..205
Chapter 54—To Light A Fire 207

Chapter 55—Another Rival Goes Down 211
Chapter 56—Outside Looking In..215
Chapter 57—The Hardest Part...218

PART VI—RECREATION

Chapter 58—Needing Respite 224
Chapter 59—Salaama Times...227
Chapter 60—The Teacher 232
Chapter 61—Wonders of Africa 234
Chapter 62—Land on Pause 239
Chapter 63—Football Without Pads 244
Chapter 64—Backyard Monolith..247
Chapter 65—Snow on the Equator 249
Chapter 66—Above the Clouds 251
Chapter 67—Fishing for Souls, Not Crocodiles 256

PART VII—AFTERMATH

Chapter 68—Checkmating A Bishop...262
Chapter 69—Reflections from Afar...264
Chapter 70—Hard Landings..266
Chapter 71—Desperation Return...269
Chapter 72—Choices Made 273
Chapter 73—Influencing..276
Chapter 74—External Forces...279
Chapter 75—Kwaheri Jackson 282
Chapter 76—Acknowledgements 284

Kenya Ethnic Map- 1974 – adapted from the
U.S. Central Intelligence Agency

PROLOGUE

Jackson's Kenya brings together two of the most important influences in my young adult life - my time in Kenya in the early 1970s, and my interaction with my Kenyan cook Jackson, who greatly shaped my view of Kenya and Africa. Not only was Jackson a great mentor for me, but his energy and joy of life were infectious. This book is a description of my work and of the Kenya I experienced with Jackson.

I served as a volunteer with the U.S. Peace Corps in Kenya from 1970-74. Fellow Wisconsin volunteer, George Roemer, lived with me for two years and worked with me for three years. His fiancée, Susan (Sue) Nicolai, arrived from Wisconsin in 1971, married George in Kenya, and lived with us during the second year. George and I were animal husbandry officers, first with the Ministry of Agriculture, and later with the Ministry of Lands and Settlement, in the former "White Highlands" in Western Province. Our work covered 19 farmer re-settlement areas called "schemes" located on either side of the Nzoia River.

George and I hired Jackson Sikolia as our cook shortly after we arrived on site. We lived in a former colonial settler house called Bettington. After George and Sue married and moved to Soy Village, I moved to Tongaren Village, the district headquarters for my settlement scheme area, where I lived for a year. Jackson moved with me. He also maintained a farm where his family lived.

Jackson's Kenya is intended to be an "honest book," covering both the ups and downs of my experience. It explains my travel dream, the process of becoming a Peace Corps volunteer in Kenya, my life at Bettington and Tongaren, my work experience, my major travel adventures, and my reflections after returning to the United States. The book is informative, serious, and sometimes humorous.

In the end, my Kenya Peace Corps experience was one of the best things I ever did. It set the tone for the rest of my life. I fell in love with the people of Kenya. It has been quite flattering for me, that, on later returns to Kenya, several people have asked me to move back.

I referred to most people in the book by their last names after introducing them. However, I referred to Jackson, George, and Sue by their first names because they were the three people closest to me throughout my time in Kenya. I apologize for the many anecdotes I felt I needed to include, called "asides" by one of my proofreaders, that sometimes proved difficult to organize. Although I have documents, notes, letters, and a reasonably good memory from my time in Kenya, I provided references necessary to back up my information, or to include new ideas or data.

PART I—WELCOME TO THE PEACE CORPS

Chapter 1—Dreaming of the Nile

President Kennedy proposed the Peace Corps during his campaign in 1960. Although I was only 12 years old at the time, I was intrigued by the idea. I wanted to travel. I had a growing curiosity about the world. Over time, I developed a desire to help people and learn another language. The Peace Corps provided the opportunity for me to do all those things.

My dream of travel apparently started early. Mom told me that, in my diapers, I crawled out of the house on our farm and down the driveway. As soon as I learned to walk, the neighbors found me on the road and brought me back home.

I attended a one-room school for all my eight elementary school years. By about the third grade, I was staring at the maps of the world that the teacher pulled down in front of the room for the sixth graders. I learned about and dreamed of places I wanted to go, things I wanted to see. I distinctly remember the River Nile, Lake Victoria, and Mount Everest. The teacher showed pictures of the pyramids, the Taj Mahal, and the Parthenon.

During my first years in elementary school, however, I did not believe I would someday see those dream places. Close family and neighbors either farmed or worked in a factory. Relatives who did travel left the community. They were too far away to influence me.

With crayons, I drew imaginary, properly colored maps. There was blue for water, green for lowlands and brown for mountains. Santiago, a name that caught my attention, was always my favorite capital city. I still have some of those maps.

My parents bought a set of Compton's Encyclopedias. We had old copies of *National Geographic* around the house. Both expanded my young horizons. My travel adventures started in books and magazines.

One day, when I was in the seventh grade, a young man named Frederick Jacoby, a member of my church, came to our grade school to show slides of his recent military tour to Antarctica. The slides showed a lot of snow and ice, nothing new or particularly interesting to me. However, the realization that someone from my community, someone I could reach out and touch, could somehow travel to the bottom of the world, suddenly changed my life. From then on, it was not a question of if, but how and when I would see the world.

I have graciously thanked Jacoby more than once. "One never knows what a life-changing influence somebody might have on a young person in the room," I told him. Jacoby spent his career as a teacher. I am sure he probably inspired many of his students in large ways.

Although my career intentions did include becoming a farmer, and even a baseball player, the travel dream was never out of my sight as I matured. In 1966, I enrolled at the University of Wisconsin at Madison in agriculture with the Peace Corps in the back of my mind. The Vietnam War loomed large over most young men of draft age like me. Fortunately, by the time the military drew my draft number of 63 in a birthdate lottery, making it likely I would be drafted, I had already applied to the Peace Corps.

CHAPTER 2—HOW ABOUT GOING TO KENYA?

I initially applied to the Peace Corps in 1969 and was accepted for a position in South America. I requested South America in part because I wanted to learn Spanish. I was frankly surprised at how quickly I was accepted.

I have always heard that only about one in five Peace Corps applicants will end up in the field. The Peace Corps will reject applicants that it deems unqualified, of course. However, some applicants will end up choosing not to go. The application process can take six months. By the end of that time, many applicants, often recent college graduates, have moved on to other things. Perhaps they either found a job or a spouse, entered graduate school, or just changed their minds. It is important to apply well ahead of time.

For some applicants, there is just not a good fit with Peace Corps job offerings. For some, there are health concerns. For others, the idealism or altruism of the opportunity is overcome by a fear of the unknown. There are many reasons for not applying for or joining the Peace Corps.

When my advisor at the university, Dr. David Wieckert, asked me early in my senior year in 1969 what my plans were after graduation, I mentioned that I was joining the Peace Corps. "Where are you going?" he asked.

"South America," I replied. "The Peace Corps has not given me a specific country yet, but I want a Spanish-speaking one. And I have not contacted my draft board yet."

"How about going to Kenya?" Wieckert asked. The university had a contract with Peace Corps Kenya. Included were incentives. There would be an application for an occupational deferment from the military for those who needed it, introductory Swahili language training on campus, and a four-credit course in international development that would serve as credits for my dairy science major.

"Some of your classmates might also be going," Wieckert continued. I surely needed the deferment because of my draft number, and the four credits were exactly what I needed to fulfill my Dairy Science Department requirement.

"Give me a week to think about it," I replied.

One week later, I told Wieckert I could go to Kenya. What I had known initially about Kenya was that it was a major tourist destination with exotic wild animals, had recently gotten its independence from Britain, and exported coffee and tea. I used my week to do more research on Kenya. I would not learn the Spanish I wanted, nor French, Arabic, or another major international language. But I liked what I saw about Kenya. Compared to most countries, Kenya looked like a paradise for a volunteer. If the Peace Corps experience did not go well, there were plenty of other things to take in.

Six University of Wisconsin-Madison volunteers from the 1970 graduating class were recruited - George Roemer, Dan Dunn, Mark Marquardt, Dennis Syth, Don Hoffman, and me. An FBI agent soon interviewed our neighbors as part of a background check. I got a

2-A occupational deferment from military service just days before President Nixon ended those deferments in April 1970.

I was introduced to an assistant dean in the College of Agriculture, Dr. Lee Swan, a former Peace Corps trainer who worked with Kenya training groups in Milwaukee in the mid-1960s. He organized the Kenya contract with Wisconsin. Swan and I lived just ten miles apart later in life. Dr. Bernard Easterday, a veterinary professor who spent time in Kenya in the 1950s, assisted with on-campus orientation. Stafford Kay, and a Kenyan whose name I do not remember, taught us basic Swahili at brown-bag lunches. The international development course, taught by various professors including Dr. William Thiesenhusen from the Land Tenure Center, was enlightening.

CHAPTER 3—UNDOING
THE UGLY AMERICAN

When President Kennedy formally established the Peace Corps in 1961, the idea was not new. Representative Henry Reuss of Wisconsin proposed a "Point Four Youth" program in the late 1950s (www.history.com/news/8-little-known-facts-about-the-peace-corps). Minnesota Senator Hubert Humphrey coined the name "Peace Corps" in his proposal for such an organization in 1960. Even Walter Reuther, the long-time president of the United Auto Workers Union, lobbied Kennedy for such an organization (Wikipedia).

The 1958 novel *The Ugly American* by Eugene Burdick and William Lederer highlighted American diplomatic failures in Southeast Asia (Wikipedia). The Peace Corps idea was heavily influenced by that book. The Peace Corps was, therefore, established in part to help offset diplomatic problems. I would add that the Peace Corps was a positive counterbalance to decades of American military interventionism and obnoxious tourists! I was told more than once by my hosts in Kenya how much they admired the willingness of young American volunteers to leave the comforts of home in the greatest country on earth to work in often-challenging conditions, and to help complete strangers at their level and on their turf.

A huge benefit of the Peace Corps was that it created in those young Americans who served an acceptance, respect, and perspective for things foreign that they would not have learned at home. Even today, it does not take me long to discern that a stranger I have just met has been out in the world in one form or another. I once told a young man after a brief conversation that he would be a good candidate for the Peace Corps. He looked and me and laughed. "How did you know?" he said. "I've already been in the Peace Corps! I was going to say the same thing to you!"

CHAPTER 4—CORPS VALUES

From its inception, the Peace Corps attempted to recruit volunteers who would succeed and make the organization and the United States proud. It did not want to deal with potential problem cases in the field. The recruitment and training processes were, therefore, points of selection or deselection.

Training in the 1960s sometimes took place on Native American reservations or in inner cities in the United States. Recruits had to go through a period of basic physical training. One Peace Corps Kenya group in 1968 trained in Bismarck, North Dakota, with part of their cross-cultural training including live-ins with Lakota families on the Standing Rock Reservation. Recruits were required to milk cows, cut (sort) cattle with horses, drive tractors, and bale hay (Swahili on the Prairie, David Asher Goldenberg, https://vimeo.com/403916814).

In some training groups in Milwaukee for Peace Corps Kenya in the mid-1960s, the goal was to eliminate half of the recruits. Letters were shoved under hotel room doors during the night at crucial points in the training process to inform recruits if they had passed on to the next round or were going home (conversations with Lee Swan).

The acrimony against the Peace Corps became so great at one

point that a group of former volunteers and failed recruits advocated for the dissolution of the organization (Lee Swan). It was eventually decided that rigorous deselection was counterproductive, and that boot camps or training under conditions that supposedly looked like the Third World had little or nothing to do with success as a volunteer.

I had always heard that several congressmen and senators, especially on the conservative side, did not like the idea of the Peace Corps. In the more extreme corners of government, foreign policy approaches to less-developed countries seemed to be limited to doing business with them, telling them about Jesus, or invading them to fix their politics. Congressman Otto Passman, a Democrat from Louisiana, was such a strong opponent of foreign aid, including the Peace Corps, that he was called "Otto the Terrible." (Wikipedia). Presidential candidate Richard Nixon once called the Peace Corps "a haven for draft-dodgers." The Peace Corps was sometimes referred to as a "junket." In Spanish, the joke about *Cuerpo de Paz* (Peace Corps) was to call it "*cuerpo de paseo*" (vacation corps) or "*cuerpo en paz*" (body in peace).

In the end, however, Nixon actually saved the Peace Corps by partnering it with VISTA (Volunteers in Service to America), also known as the "domestic Peace Corps," into a new organization called "ACTION." ACTION was put under a different funding stream less vulnerable to the whims of Congress (Wikipedia). We were told during training in 1970 that the total annual budget of the Peace Corps, including the cost of maintaining 6,000 to 10,000 volunteers in the field, plus administration and recruiting, was less than half the price of one nuclear submarine. *I have not been able to find the cost of a nuclear submarine at the time.* The Peace Corps budget for Fiscal Year 1972 was reduced from $90 million to $60 million and the number of volunteers reduced from 9,000 to 5,800 (*wikipedia.org/ wiki/Joseph_Blatchford*).

The Peace Corps in the 1960s was often unable to match volunteers' skills with their appropriate assignments. There were too many liberal arts applicants and not enough science or technical applicants to fill host country requests. I recall that, during our in-country training in Kenya, we met a psychology major working in agriculture extension. He was not well-matched nor happy with his assignment, and eventually went home. Although some volunteers were able to adapt well, putting a volunteer in a position that he or she was ill-qualified for was not fair to the volunteer nor to the host country.

By 1970, many of the recruits had bachelors' or technical degrees appropriate for their positions. Science, math, and health were usually the largest recruitment areas. Agriculture and engineering was also a large portion of the roughly 350 volunteers in Kenya at that time. A bachelor's degree was almost a must for younger volunteers in terms of maturity and ability to cope with the complexity of the assignment. Many volunteers had additional relevant experience in their fields. I had a bachelors' degree in dairy science coupled with a dairy farm upbringing.

The University of Wisconsin in Madison contributed 20 agriculture volunteers for Kenya between 1970-72. The Madison campus has historically been the second largest recruiter in the total number of Peace Corps volunteers with 3,279 after the University of California-Berkeley with 3,671 (Bill Novak, *Wisconsin State Journal*, Feb. 21, 2018).

As of 2020, about 240,000 Americans have served in the Peace Corps (PeaceCorps.gov). My Peace Corps "volunteer number" in 1970 was 281662. I am not sure if it was an application number or something else. A recent volunteer I know had a number over 100,000,000.

We were told during staging and training that there would be challenges, both physical and psychological. Volunteers would have to overcome adversity. Primitive living conditions, tropical weather, insects, dirty water, and unsafe food would be compounded by cultural differences, poverty, ignorance, and corruption. The Peace Corps would not be in Kenya if everything in the country was going right. As a farm boy, I felt I might be better prepared than most to handle adversity. "S*** happens regularly on Wisconsin dairy farms!" I thought to myself.

CHAPTER 5—THE PHILADELPHIA STORY

Forty-eight volunteers, including the six of us from Wisconsin, arrived at the Sylvania Hotel in Philadelphia on June 17, 1970 for nine days of staging before flying to Kenya for training. For several of us, including me, it was our first time to board a plane. For me, it was just the second time I ever stayed in a hotel.

For simplicity, I will refer to our group as "volunteers" from this point on, although we were technically trainees. We would not officially become volunteers until a swearing-in ceremony at the United States Embassy in Kenya after training.

What I conveniently called the "agriculture and engineering group" (officially Kenya Ag VI) was actually composed of a mixture of volunteers in the following areas: water development (21), veterinary lab technicians (2), agronomy (2), horticulture (1), squatter settlement (8), dairy (3), fisheries (2), agricultural finance (2), smallholder beef (2), range management (1), urban planning (1), and medical illustration (1). There were also two spouses in the group. George Roemer, Dennis Syth, and I were the dairy volunteers.

There were preliminary training sessions, last-minute medical and dental checks, and evaluations for each volunteer regarding his motivation. When asked why I was joining the Peace Corps, I told the committee of three in the room about my dreams to see the world and to help people. "Are you trying to avoid Vietnam?" one of them asked.

"That would be my third reason," I replied nervously.

"Thank you for your honesty," one said. "Welcome to the Peace Corps!"

At one of the sessions in Philadelphia, an economist talked at length about development parameters and other macro-economic concepts. I appreciated the perspective, but I sensed a disconnection between the economic philosophy and what I was going to be expected to do in the field. I kept thinking to myself, "What does this have to do with feeding cows, planting corn or marketing vegetables?" Throughout staging, I noticed that many of the Peace Corps staff we dealt with were Ivy League types, a world apart from my Wisconsin farm background. I noted that, although the Peace Corps was now recruiting technical people, it was still managed by staff with liberal arts backgrounds.

We were given encouragement and time off by the Peace Corps to visit historical sites in the city. I saw Independence Hall, the Liberty Bell, Benjamin Franklin's grave, and the U.S. Mint. I was surprised to learn that the mint made currency for dozens of foreign countries.

CHAPTER 6—COASTAL LEARNING

After staging, we flew to Nairobi via Boston, Lisbon, Rome, and Entebbe. The long flights and jet lag caused us to immediately "crash" on our beds when we got to our hotel. We later visited the Nairobi game park. I was fascinated by the idea that there could be wild game, including lions, just a few hundred yards from downtown Nairobi, separated only by a fence on the opposite side of Uhuru Highway. After a couple of days, we took the night train to Mombasa.

The in-country training in Mombasa included five weeks of Swahili and cultural training, followed by a three-week technical training tour in other parts of the country. The tour was designed to be relevant to the specific expertise of each volunteer.

The main part of Mombasa City is an island connected to the mainland by causeways or bridges. During Swahili training, volunteers lived with families on Mombasa island or on the north coast. I lived on the north coast in Kisauni with three other volunteers, sponsored by two host families. One host was a teacher named Mohammed Salim Ahmed. The other was an accountant at the port of Mombasa named Al'min Muhsin.

Training sessions took place at the New Sea Breezes Hotel on the south coast. To reach the hotel, the four of us in Kisauni had to cross a floating bridge to the main island and then take the Likoni Ferry across the port entrance. We walked from there to the hotel. Muhsin drove us in his car back and forth to the ferry and provided breakfast. Salim housed us and provided dinner.

Sheik Haider was in charge of placing volunteers with families. My living situation worked out well, although a few of the other living situations were crowded and uncomfortable. One volunteer had to switch families because he was sharing a bedroom with multiple children and not getting any sleep. I remember the sheik and a Jewish volunteer having some political disagreements!

Dinner at Salim's was entirely a male event. We did not sit on the floor, as may have been customary, but had a table and chairs. Although women did the cooking, they were not seen. Salim's small son brought the food to us. Food was served in large communal bowls or plates with serving spoons. After washing our hands, we ate with our right hand using individual plates. Being left-handed, I had several adjustments to make for Muslim culture. I was surprised that Salim never introduced his wife during the first three weeks we were living there, even though she was certainly present behind the scenes.

At the end of the third week, Salim took us to what I thought to be his weekend home in Kilifi, farther up the north coast. It was there we finally met his wife. She was there with their daughter. Salim's wife was a beautiful woman who spoke excellent English. Like Salim, she was a teacher.

Salim took the four of us to a Muslim wedding. The men gathered in one large room and the women in another. All male attendees were dressed in white robes and Muslim caps or turbans, except for us volunteers. I joked that we were never told by the Peace Corps to come equipped with the proper Muslim wedding attire!

As we waited for the ceremony, I noticed that one young man was nervously pacing about. I asked Salim why the man was so nervous. "He is the groom," Salim replied. "He has never met the bride!" Salim went on to explain that the families knew each other, of course, and that the groom had probably "viewed" his future bride in the past. As was the custom, this was an arranged marriage. There was no dating.

In Mombasa in 1970, the process of sorting out volunteers during in-country training to see if they remained fit for the Peace Corps was specifically stated as "self-deselection." I still have a memo that mentions it. We were subjected to small group sessions of about a half-dozen volunteers with a psychologist. In the back of my mind, I recalled something in the 1960s called a "T-group" or "encounter group" used as therapy to help people communicate better.

One of the sessions seemed to get sinister. The psychologist set up a situation where I was pitted against another volunteer. The volunteer became angry at me, and I became angry at the psychologist. "This guy is testing me," I thought. "Is this how they conduct self-deselection?" I was afraid that they were trying to break me in order to send me home. Peace Corps was the beginning of my dream. I was determined that it was not going to end here. I refused to be manipulated. I suddenly shouted at the psychologist. "I don't know what you are trying to do here! I have nothing against this man. I'm staying!" No one ever questioned me again.

A few days later, one of my best friends in training, a man from Michigan who was assigned to a different session, came sadly up to me. He was going home. "I guess I wasn't meant to be a Peace Corps volunteer," he said. I tried to question him about what had happened. I wanted him to stick it out, but the decision had already been made.

During training, we received several vaccinations. Dr. Sobeck, the Peace Corps doctor, was on hand in Mombasa. Before, during and after my two Peace Corps experiences, I was vaccinated multiple times for smallpox, yellow fever, cholera, typhoid, typhus, diphtheria, tetanus, tuberculosis, hepatitis A and B, rabies boosters, and influenza. We took an aralen tablet once a week in Kenya to prevent malaria. During my lifetime, I estimated that I have received at least 80 total vaccinations. None have injured me in any way that I can detect, and several may have saved or extended my life. I have never had malaria, but contracted hepatitis A in South America after I carelessly let my vaccination expire.

Finally, toward the end of training, the dairy, beef, and agronomy volunteers got to choose their respective work sites. We deferred first to the women in the mix. They decided to stay closer to Nairobi. Margaret Schuette took a position with Veterinary School Faculty in Kabete. Tammy Taylor chose the poultry extension position in the Ruiru-Kabete area. John Ewing also went to the Veterinary School.

I volunteered next, asking for the location farthest from Nairobi, not knowing exactly where that was at the time. It turned out to be the Bungoma District Settlement Schemes in Western Province. My reason for choosing it had nothing to do with the specifics of the location. After training, I was rather tired of being "managed" by the Peace Corps, so I wanted to be as far out of sight as possible.

Dennis Syth took the Nyeri position north of Nairobi. George Roemer got the Kakamega District Settlement Schemes in Western Province. He and I would live together and work on either side of the Nzoia River that split the two districts. Don Hoffman, and Bruce Hackmeister from Kansas, were assigned to the Lanet Beef Research Station outside of Nakuru. Dan Dunn went to the Agriculture Finance Corporation in Eldoret. Mark Marquardt was assigned to a squatter settlement in Eastern Province. He would later move into the Ministry of Agriculture in Nairobi.

There were no Peace Corps agriculture extension positions in the arid northern 80% of the country. But a few water engineers had been posted in those areas to dig wells. The north was largely occupied by nomadic herders and was often dangerous because of *shifta* (bandits), especially near the Ethiopian and Somali borders. The Northern Frontier District or NFD, later called Northeastern Province, was especially notorious.

We all passed our Swahili language training. I achieved an FSI (Foreign Service Institute) proficiency level 2, which I understood to mean that I had a command of basic conversation plus some use of the subjunctive and conditional tenses. The range for the test was 0 to 5. In Mombasa, one needed an FSI 1+ to pass. I learned that a level 4 would be a native speaker and a level 5 would be a linguist. The Peace Corps, the largest language trainer in the world, teaches more than 350 languages (peacecorps.gov/multimedia).

I, for one, did not feel comfortable with my Swahili after only five weeks, but enjoyed learning the language. My enthusiasm must have shown. During one of my classes, I attempted to explain with my limited Swahili how a horse and a donkey could mate to produce a mule. I am not sure how that came up. We were "aggies," you know, concerned about such things! There were no women in the class.

At the end of training in Mombasa, there was a goat roast in our honor. A goat roast is a special occasion in Kenya, less important than a cow roast but certainly greater than a chicken roast. It was my first ever goat roast. The goat was tasty but tough as rope. I remember asking for toothpicks or floss to remove the stringy meat from my teeth. Despite the inconveniences, it was a festive occasion. The hotel marked the first time that I ever tasted mangoes, papayas, and passion fruit. I could not imagine any fruit as good as a mango, so I ate three of them the first time.

After the party, we ended up spending a night at the New Sea Breezes Hotel. I remember lying around the pool at midnight watching the sky. There were the usual shooting stars and a satellite buzzing across the sky. It was the first time I ever saw the Southern Cross constellation.

CHAPTER 7—LINGUA FRANCA

D airy science majors at the University of Wisconsin had to take the expected departmental and supportive courses to meet requirements of the degree. There was always room for electives. I took history, anthropology, journalism, and Spanish, among others.

At the beginning of each semester, we joked about which unusual elective we might take. One of those potential electives was a Swahili language and culture course. Each semester some of my colleagues and I wondered if this were finally the opportunity to fit that Swahili course into our schedules. We just laughed about it! Little did we know that a few of us in a couple of years would be speaking the language and living in the culture. The lesson here is to respect all things. What you might joke about carelessly today might be a serious part of your life tomorrow!

Swahili or *Kiswahili* is a language originating from the coast of East Africa that combines basic Bantu structure with many Arabic nouns. "*Sawahili*" is an Arabic word for "of the coast" (*ismailimail. blog/2014/12/24/the-word-swahili-is-from-arabic*). Swahili was originally written in Arabic letters, then changed to Roman letters after Europeans arrived. It is a trade language used primarily among peoples in Tanzania, Kenya, Uganda, Rwanda, Burundi, the eastern Congo, and the borders of Zambia and Mozambique. Swahili, like Hausa in West Africa, is an important, indigenous pan-African language that is offered on many large university campuses around the world.

The basic Swahili we learned in training served us well "upcountry" where people primarily spoke their tribal language while using Swahili to communicate between tribes. On the coast, however, Swahili is the primary language. Zanzibar Swahili is still considered to be the language standard. When I traveled to the coast, people understood me, but I had trouble understanding them. I eventually understood upcountry Swahili well enough to listen to local radio, but not the Zanzibar Swahili used on the BBC.

I learned that several authors have translated parts or all of Shakespeare into Swahili, including Tanzania's first president, Julius Nyerere, who was considered a Swahili scholar (Global South Studies, University of Virginia). I still have not read Shakespeare in Swahili but would surely like to.

When I later traveled to Arabic-speaking countries, I heard numbers and occasional nouns that were similar to Swahili. Swahili typically adds a vowel to the end of a word that ends in a consonant. Swahili also borrowed a few words from other languages besides Arabic, like *mesa* (table) from Portuguese and *shule* (school) from German. A few words from Swahili have slipped into English like *safari, harambee* (all pull together or self-help), *kwanzaa* (first fruits or first born), and *malaika* (angel), now used as a girl's name. We can thank *The Lion King* movie more recently for *simba* (lion), *rafiki* (friend), *pumbaa* (foolish) and *hakuna matata* (no trouble or worry). Learning Swahili for me in 1970, however, coming from an English-European language background, meant I had to learn an entirely new system of communication with all new words and sentence structure.

In Bantu languages, the prefix has an important meaning. I once heard this explanation from a Ugandan colleague. Using Uganda as the example, *ganda* is the root for the people, a large tribe in Uganda, made up of many clans. *U-ganda* is the place. *Ki-ganda* is the language or culture, like *Ki-swahili*. *Lu-ganda* is also used for the language. *Ba-ganda* are the people. *Mu-ganda* is the person. *Mwa-ganda* or *Mwana-ganda* is a member of the Baganda people. *Bu-ganda* is the nation or kingdom. I hope I got this all straight! In Swahili, prefixes also denote singular and plural of some nouns, and verb tenses. Examples would be *mtu* (person), *watu* (people), *kiti* (chair), and *viti* (chairs).

All languages have beautiful expressions for things within their cultural and historical contexts. Even today, 50 years since my first exposure to Swahili, there are Swahili words and expressions I remember that better describe situations than my best English. For several years after I returned to the U.S., Swahili expressions would immediately come to mind. I also had Swahili conversations in my sleep.

Swahili greetings are polite and expected to be used before anything else is discussed. The common one is *"jambo, habari gani?"* (hello, what is the news/how are you?). Several *habaris* may be asked about your health, family, etc. One is expected to respond to greetings in a positive way, normally *"mzuri sana"* (very well) until the proper protocol is complete, even if you have a broken leg or other obvious problems. After that, one can discuss whatever issues may be on one's mind. Multiple or repeated greetings were also used in Kiluhya, the tribal language used where I lived. I cannot imagine New York City taxi drivers going through a set of polite greetings before shouting at you from their car windows about something!

I do not remember any cuss or swear words in Swahili. One can find them online (cusstionary.com//Swahili). Cuss words were the first German I learned at home, for instance, when my father was kicked by a cow. I have retained several Spanish cuss words from my Paraguay days. I thank my Swahili instructors and my Kenyan friends for not using such words. George Roemer told me that he recalled using the expression "*mavi ya kuku*" (chicken s***).

I have noticed, over time, that as American English expressions have become more common in Kenya, the F-word may be used. Of likely German origin, it is probably America's greatest linguistic contribution to the world's lexicon!

CHAPTER 8—CROSSING THE EQUATOR

After Mombasa, the agriculture volunteers embarked on their job-specific, three-week technical training tour. Our group visited the Kabete Veterinary School, the Uplands Bacon Factory (since closed), the Lanet Beef Research Station, the Egerton Technical College, the Kakamega Agriculture Research Station, the Kenya Seed Company, and a few small-scale and large-scale farms. These visits gave us a better idea of the size and scope of agricultural research and industry in the country. It was during the tour that we met Peter Petges, an extension volunteer from Illinois who was already working in the Kakamega Settlement Schemes.

Egerton College, like several of the three-year technical colleges at the time, is now a university. In 1970, Kenya had one public university based in Nairobi. Today there are more than 20. There are now close to 30 private universities (Wikipedia).

The technical training tour was our first trip to western Kenya and our first time to cross the equator on land. Mombasa and Nairobi are both south of the equator, while Eldoret and Kitale, near where George and I would be working, are north of the equator.

The equator sign along the highway at Molo between Nakuru

and Eldoret was constructed of wood. It portrayed a map of Africa with the equator line drawn through Kenya. When I crossed the equator again in 1987, the wooden panel had been replaced with a metal one.

In 1987, it appeared to me that the sign had been moved several feet from its original location. Perhaps it was just a figment of my imagination, or perhaps the true location of equator had indeed been re-surveyed. The equator sign at Meru was moved more than a half mile after a new survey (*African Standard*, August 9, 2018). Contrary to popular opinion, the equator is not a yellow line circumventing the earth!

There is another sign just north of Kisumu, the one featured on the cover. I was told that, after the metal panel was installed, a local farmer came at night and stole it. Thinking that it would be a good substitute for *mabati* (corrugated metal), he installed it on the roof of his house. The person who told me the story figured the man probably did not understand the significance of the equator map he now displayed on his house. The sign was easily spotted by police and returned to the roadside, and the man was fined. I was not able to verify this story, but it sounds plausible.

We each took turns driving a Volkswagen minibus on the technical training tour. For most of us, this was our first experience driving on the left side of the road. Driving on the left is not so hard, but making the turns is where one gets messed up. About one-third of the population of the world drives on the left, including many of the former British colonies (businessinsider.com.au).

On the last leg back to Nairobi, it was my turn to drive. While driving through Naivasha on the main highway, I had a minor accident. There was a festival of some kind in the city. An older white man pulled his car out in front of me, breaking the headlight on the minibus. Kenyan police quickly came upon the scene on foot. They immediately saluted the old man. "Who was this old white guy that we collided with?" all of us volunteers wondered at once. The man got out of his car, apologized for the accident, gave us his contact information, and said that we should send him the bill. He turned out to be the first-class magistrate of Naivasha, a senior judge. He was one of many British judges that Kenya kept on after independence to help transition the nation's legal system. The man was also very drunk.

CHAPTER 9—REMINDERS
OF DESTRUCTION

W e were officially sworn in as Peace Corps Volunteers at the U.S. Embassy in Nairobi by the ambassador, with an oath of allegiance to the United States. We were now federal employees. The ambassador, Robinson McIlvaine, was a career diplomat on his last assignment before retirement (*New York Times* Obituaries, June 27, 2001). He had served in Portugal, Congo, Benin, and Guinea before Kenya. The embassy was in a nondescript office building in downtown Nairobi with the usual security for the time.

On a later occasion, I met Ambassador McIlvaine on the street, reminding him who I was. We had a brief, pleasant conversation. He was a mild-mannered gentleman. One of his successors, Smith Hempstone, was not so mild-mannered, at least not with the Kenyan government. Hempstone was an outspoken proponent of increased democracy in Kenya and a thorn in the side of President Moi's administration (New York Time Obituaries, November 30, 2006; also *Rogue Ambassador: An African Memoir*, book by Smith Hempstone).

The embassy was later moved to another office building that I happened to visit in 1987. That building was bombed by Al Qaeda terrorists in 1998, killing more than 200 people. Most of the deaths occurred in a hospital next door. The new embassy, now located outside of the downtown area, is heavily fortified.

It is scary to think of the buildings I have been in that were later attacked or destroyed. In addition to the embassy, my Kenya list includes the International Airport Terminal, which accidentally burned in 2013, and the Westgate Mall, which was attacked by Al-Shabab terrorists, also in 2013 (Wikipedia).

Another building from my past, this one in the United States, was bombed in August of 1970. At the end of our technical training tour, we heard about the bombing of the Physics Building at the University of Wisconsin in Madison where military-related research during the Vietnam War was funded. A post-doctoral researcher was killed. My first university class period in the fall of 1966, a discussion section, was held on the fourth floor on the side of the building that was blown off.

PART II—
BETTINGTON

CHAPTER 10—WHO ARE YOU?

At the end of August in 1970, the volunteers were ready to report to their sites and start work. George Roemer and I were issued a single vehicle in my name, a white Mini Moke, to start our work. A second Moke would be issued shortly.

The Mini Moke, manufactured by Austin Morris, looked like a glorified dune buggy or golf cart. It had front-wheel drive with a transverse engine. The canvas top of the vehicle was draped over a roll bar. There were canvas sides which we never used. One had to climb over the gas tank on the left side to get into the passenger seat. Mokes were durable and gutsy vehicles that volunteers got an incredible amount of work from.

George and I were told to report to the Provincial Agriculture Office in Kakamega in Western Province. We arrived late in the day, so we spent the night in Kakamega. We were directed to the Provincial Crops Officer when we reported the next morning.

"Who are you?" the Crops Officer asked. After we explained, he fished around in his desk drawer for a letter of introduction that he remembered seeing but could not find. "Oh, you are those new *'Peace-Corpse chaps'* we were told about!" He repeated what we had already told him about being assigned to the settlement schemes at Nzoia. "I believe your positions in the Ministry will be as Animal Husbandry Officers, Grade Two." The Crops Officer then told us to report to our Peace Corps colleague, Peter Petges, in Turbo, about 45 miles to the north within George's assigned area. "You two might be sharing a house," he told us. "I will book a call to the Turbo office for you to meet Petges this afternoon," he said.

One could not just make a telephone call. It usually needed to be "booked" an hour or more in advance because there were so few lines around the western part of the country. After George and I settled in at our house, the nearest phone was about ten miles away at the Nzoia office near Hoey's Bridge Village. We would have to wait around until the call went through. Even then the connection might be bad, making it difficult to hear the other person. We were once told that a call from Hoey's Bridge to Kakamega 55 miles away would have to be routed through Nairobi, 250 miles in the opposite direction, and then back.

When George and I arrived in Turbo from Kakamega that afternoon, Petges was waiting for us. "I knew you would be here one of these days," Petges said, not referring to any specific message he may or may not have received. "You are going to live in Bettington, a former colonial house in Hoey's Bridge Scheme. Unfortunately, they just put the furniture in storage," he continued. We had to arrange to get it returned.

CHAPTER 11—CULINARY CHRONICLES

B efore we left town, George and I went to a local restaurant in Kakamega for lunch. There were about 20 items on the menu. We each ordered an item. "We are out of those today," we were told by the waiter. We chose other items. "We are out of those today," he continued each time. After going through most of the menu, we discovered that only one item was available. After the waiter left, we asked each other why the waiter did not just cut to the chase and tell us what was available. We supposed that he was too embarrassed to admit the restaurant's shortcomings. We ended up with chicken in a sauce with a side of *ugali* (doughy corn meal). We were not offered any silverware, being expected to eat most food by hand. I asked for a spoon anyway. The meal was good.

For some reason, nonetheless, I thought of a joke that was told during training. Having a fly in one's soup is a metaphor for an unpleasant surprise. The idea developed into a joke about dietary adaptation in the Peace Corps. The length of stay and durability of a volunteer in country can be judged by how he regards having a fly in his soup in a restaurant. When the volunteer first arrives and finds a fly in his soup, he gets up in disgust and leaves the restaurant. After six months in country, the volunteer picks the fly out and eats the soup. After one year in country, the volunteer eats the fly with the soup. After two years in country, the volunteer asks for more flies!

Not all food was safe or palatable. We would find out, especially during our first year in country, that our naïve digestive systems and tastes were occasionally challenged. I got serious food poisoning four times in four years, once from poorly cooked chicken on a farm visit and once from bad *chai* (tea with milk) in a local restaurant. I do not remember how the other two cases occurred. The first time was the worst. I was off from work for about three days. Each subsequent time was less severe, perhaps indicating an increased immunity on my part.

We were issued iodine tablets for water purification. Using these on farm visits would have been impractical and insulting to our hosts. Bottled water was not available. In any case, I was seldom offered water on the farm and usually declined to drink it.

At our new home at Bettington, we had to boil and then filter our water through charcoal. At the 6,000-foot altitude where we lived, water boiled at about 200 degrees Fahrenheit, necessitating a few extra minutes of boiling to achieve the same sanitizing effect as 212 degrees. When I moved to Tongaren and purchased river water, I was even more vigilant about boiling and filtering.

A world traveler friend once told me that she would drink the tap water the first morning in each new country and not eat breakfast. If there were no symptoms, her system was then inoculated, and she could then eat lunch. No doctor I know of would ever give such advice, but I also heard about this from an old Kenyan woman.

Chapter 12—Too Much of a Good Thing

George and I settled in at Bettington. The house was made of red brick. The living room and dining room each had fireplaces. The two main bedrooms each had their own toilets and bathtubs. There were two additional smaller bedrooms for guests or employees. The kitchen had a cast-iron woodstove. There was a kerosene refrigerator.

There was a generator for electricity as well as an outdoor cistern for water. George and I ran the generator only for special occasions. It was powered by an ancient and oily Wisconsin brand engine. Every time we fired it up, we got oil splashed on us. We largely depended on Petromax kerosene pressure lamps and candles for our evening lighting.

A pump at the river brought water to the cistern. We found a *fundi* (expert/mechanic) to occasionally maintain the pump. A hand pump was then used to lift water up into a gravity tank. Rain gutters also channeled water into a large, corrugated water tank at the corner of the house. We had to carry water into the house for cooking, bath, and toilet. Neighbors had emptied the rain tank. When we first arrived, we had to bring well water from a neighbor and store it in one of the bathtubs.

Outside, there was a separate two-car garage and a servant's quarters. There was a half-acre of lawn and garden with flowers and flowering shrubs including cannas, four-foot poinsettias, and a frangipani tree with fragrant blossoms. Tall Eucalyptus trees lined the driveway.

Bettington represented what I thought was very exotic housing for a couple of measly Peace Corps volunteers. It was almost too much of a good thing! The Peace Corps water engineers also lived in several former colonial houses nearby. There was no other so-called "acceptable" housing in the rural areas. Local housing was either too much or too little, it seemed. The Peace Corps had previously provided two prefab wooden houses for volunteers in the Lumakanda Village area, one for Bob Sherwood and one for Petges.

Local Kenyans suddenly showed up offering to cook or work around the house. Older volunteers like Petges and Larry Day, who lived nearby, told us we could easily get a cook for about 80 Kenya shillings (Ksh) per month, roughly $12. The upcountry volunteer salary for volunteers was 1200 Ksh, or about $168 per month. Vehicle maintenance and *petrol* (gasoline) were covered by the Peace Corps.

In the British system, there are 20 shillings in a pound. Kenya adopted shillings as the national currency but did not use pounds. Kenyans referred to shillings as "*shilingi*." The British in Kenya, as in Britain, often referred colloquially to shillings as "*bob*" and pounds as "*quid*."

George and I decided to hire a cook, preferably with experience working for other *wazungu* (white people, foreigners). We passed up an offer from a less-experienced man named *Mzee* Pews because we heard there was a great cook available working for another volunteer in the area.

The title *Mzee* (old or old person or respected old man) was typically reserved for older men, often with a beard. Kenyan men usually did not or could not grow good beards until they got older. Peace Corps men were told not to grow beards because it would be an insult to older men. George grew one anyway. I was called "*Mzee*" on a few occasions, but rejected the title immediately, deferring instead to just "Otto" or "*Bwana* (mister) Otto." *Mzee* was also used for President Kenyatta. He was "thee *Mzee*," especially when speaking in the context of the presidency or Kenyan government.

The 6,000-foot altitude location where we lived made the local climate rather comfortable. Nairobi's altitude was about 5,500 feet. Only Mombasa at sea level and the Lake Victoria region at 3,000 feet were the only places I spent any significant time where I was at all uncomfortable. I grew up with sinus problems; in western Kenya, the high altitude and low humidity cleared my head. Kenya was climatically one of the most comfortable places I ever lived in.

CHAPTER 13—JAMBO JACKSON

Alan Johnston was a local Peace Corps volunteer living in the area who came to Kenya in 1968. He worked with co-operatives. Johnston was joined in 1969 by his fiancée, Sally, and they were married in Kenya. The Johnstons decided they no longer needed a cook and heard that we were looking for one. We heard that their cook named Jackson was highly recommended.

The Johnstons invited us to their house. Alan and Sally were very friendly. There was initial small talk about the Peace Corps and the settlement schemes. Alan talked about his accounting work with the cooperatives.

Jackson was then introduced. I distinctly remember seeing him for the first time. He was handsome and fit, about 30, with a ready smile. Jackson greeted us, "*Jambo sana, karibu!*" (hello very much, welcome). He smiled and said little else. I could see that he was sizing us up. Alan told us something to the effect that Jackson understood English but would be very good for our Swahili.

The Johnstons talked about eventually returning to the United States. "What are you going to do when you get back?" I asked them. Jackson suddenly interjected in Swahili that Alan only had a bachelors' degree while Sally had a masters. *"Nitakua mpishi wake!"* (I will be her cook), Alan joked. We all laughed.

George and I agreed to hire Jackson at 120 Ksh. It soon became apparent that Jackson would fit well. We expected to learn a lot from him. I had no idea at the time how much Jackson would mean to us, especially to me. Over time, we learned from Jackson that, before the Johnstons, he had first worked for a British settler named Baker, and then for Peace Corps volunteers Noel Morgen, Charles Pike, and Bob Sherwood.

Jackson Sikolia Murunga was born in Chekulo Village, Kabrasi Division, Kakamega District in Western Province in Kenya, about 50 miles from Bettington. He once said he thought he was born in 1936, but his birth was not registered until 1939. I found out later that he had an older sibling born in 1936 who lived only two years. Jackson thought his birthday was on December 23. Again, he did not seem sure. Many Kenyans from Jackson's generation and earlier did not have accurate information on their birthdates and ages.

Jackson's settlement farm was about 20 miles from Bettington. He and his family lived on Plot Number 127 in Lumakanda Scheme, one of the settlement schemes in Petges's and George's working areas. Lumakanda was also the name of the village within the scheme and was located between the Turbo and Kipkarren River Villages close to the Uganda Highway.

Because there was no formal rural postal delivery, Jackson's mailing address was a post office box. Most people could not afford their own postal boxes, so they received mail at a local village office or school postal box. Jackson's first postal box at Turbo was the one used by the Lumakanda Settlement Office, so mail would conveniently arrive at a location near Jackson's farm. When Jackson became chairman of the Lumakanda Cooperative Society, he used the Kipkarren River postal box that was used by the cooperative.

Jackson also told me later he did not trust having his mail handled by the settlement people.

A middle-aged man nicknamed *Mzee Pembe* (Mister Horn), who lived with us at Bettington in one of the extra rooms, worked for the postal service. He bicycled five days a week to Hoey's Bridge Village to collect mail from the post office there and deliver it the Nzoia office, a round trip of roughly 30 miles. The Nzoia office was the headquarters for the water project, the veterinary office, and the artificial insemination service. In casual conversation, we just referred to the Nzoia office as "Headquarters." I occasionally found mail at the Nzoia office for my settlement schemes and took it along on a work trip to a village center or gave it to my agriculture assistants.

Although Kenya officially adopted the metric system in 1967 (Kenya metric, thepostemail.com), the country was still transitioning from the English system in 1970. Most people, including Jackson, still referred to *maili* (mile) and *futi* (foot) when using measurements, or galoni (gallon) when referring to volume. The old white road markers were still in miles, but the newer distance signs were in kilometers. The equator signs in 1970 gave the elevation in feet. Later signs were in meters. I stayed with the English system in this book.

Jackson had two wives when George and I hired him. The first was Tina Makokha Matsasio, and the second was Angela Khalenya Litumbu. Tina had three children at the time. The first was Moses Chiluli Kenyatta Sikolia, born in 1965 and named after President Jomo Kenyatta. The second was Richard Musenjeli Sikolia, born in 1968 and named after U.S. President Richard Nixon, who had just been elected. The third was David Nabwera Sikolia, born in 1971 and named after my advisor, David Wieckert, who was visiting George and me in Kenya at the time.

Angela had no children at first, leaving Jackson to believe she was barren. That turned out not to be true. Jackson would eventually have eight children with each of his wives, plus six children out of wedlock. Jackson married a third wife later, a widow named Clementina Mukasia. They had no children together.

Jackson's parents were still alive and lived in Lumakanda when we employed him. His father, Murunga, lived to be quite old and often smoked *bhangi* (marijuana), something Jackson complained about. Jackson told me once that he was so angry about Murunga's smoking that he broke Murunga's pipe. Jackson's youngest sibling Alice repaired the pipe for her father.

Although many Kenyans I met professed membership in a western religion, traditions like polygamy were still strong. Tina was an Anglican and Angela a Catholic. Jackson never professed any religion until late in life, when he told me he had become a Catholic.

CHAPTER 14—PICTURES AND POPCORN

Not long after George and I met the Johnstons, we received an invitation to a slide show at their house. Alan and Sally had recently gone on a camera safari to one of the game parks and were putting on one of several slideshows they gave for the local Kenyans. George, Jackson, and I were present. Sally made popcorn and served a type of Kool-Aid. Alan rigged up a projector to a car battery and set up a screen outside on the lawn. About 30 Kenyans showed up. Alan later told me that none of the Kenyans had ever eaten popcorn before.

There were a lot of "oohs" and "aahs" from the crowd. I remember some of the Kenyans commenting about the lions. *"Simba kali!"* (fierce lions), they murmured. It was apparent to me that none of them had ever seen these wild animals that their country was so famous for. Foreign tourists were more likely to see the wildlife than the Kenyans.

Most wildlife lived in game parks or game reserves considerable distances from normal civilization. Some animals, like monkeys, giraffes, and leopards, could be found locally. It was likely the Kenyans at the slide show did not have the resources to visit the parks and would probably never do so in their lifetimes. Perhaps the animals were not as novel to some of them as they were to the tourists.

Perhaps similarly, I grew up within three miles of Lake Michigan, but took little interest in the recreational opportunities it offered. Yet tourists from across the region spent considerable time and money to take advantage of its amenities. To me, Lake Michigan was an unfriendly, large, frigid body of water that created raw, humid winds, lake-effect snowstorms, and late springs.

I remember a conversation with a neighbor at Bettington, a man in his forties who spoke good English. He had never been to Eldoret, a 30-mile bus ride away. "I have no idea what it looks like," he stated. I offered to take him there sometime. He never took me up on the offer.

I wondered how many people, especially the *shamba* (farm) wives, had seldom or never traveled more than a few miles from where they were born. It was the men who usually moved about taking care of business or working off the farm, while the wives took care of the children and the farm.

CHAPTER 15—THE GOOD, THE BAD, AND THE COLONIALS

W hen I arrived in Kenya in late June of 1970, it was just six-and-one-half years after Kenya's full independence from Britain on December 12, 1963. The first British colony in Sub-Saharan Africa to gain its independence was Ghana in 1957. In terms of development, Kenya should have gotten its independence earlier than 1963. The Mau Mau Rebellion, fought mostly by Kikuyus against the colonial government in Kenya in the 1950s and early 1960s, delayed that idea. Many in the white community in Kenya wished for Kenya to be a permanent white colony. That was not meant to happen. South Africa and Southern Rhodesia, ruled by whites at the time, appeared to offer that white colony option.

I wrote about the Mau Mau Rebellion for one of my course papers at Ohio University in Athens, Ohio in 1982. Ohio University was able to obtain microfiche copies of recently declassified British and American documents from the Mau Mau era. Most of the items I saw were rather mundane provincial and district officer reports. However, in combination with my other readings, I was able to understand much about the struggle. President Kenyatta, who was accused of inciting the Mau Mau Rebellion and who was then exiled near the Sudan border during the struggle, denied involvement (www.quora.com/What-was-Jomo-Kenyattas-position).

There was still a certain euphoria about independence in Kenya when I arrived. Kenyans had much hope for the future, an opportunity to build their own country on their own terms. "Nation-building" was one of the catch phrases of the time. However, the reality of African politics was already setting in. The assassination of Cabinet Minister Tom Mboya in 1969 was a serious blow to that euphoria.

Many of the colonial settlers who had previously lived in Kenya were bought out by the Kenyan government under the Settlement Fund Trustees program (Land Settlement Programs in Kenya, strategicjournals.com). The money for the buyout was a loan from the British government to the Kenyan government. Most of those settlers, already having British citizenship but born in Kenya, did not opt for Kenya citizenship, deciding instead to move to Britain, Southern Rhodesia, Australia, or elsewhere.

The settlement schemes where George and I worked in Western Province were established after independence to resettle Kenyan farmers on the former White Highlands. The region got its name because it was settled when colonization began in the early 1900s by white people from Europe, mostly from Britain, and because the altitude was around 6,000 feet. There were other colonial areas in other parts of Kenya also referred to as White Highlands.

There were numerous colonial farmhouses remaining when George and I arrived. The houses and adjoining properties were known by their former owner's names preceded by "Ex." For example, the house George, Jackson, and I lived in was usually known as "Ex-Bettington." George and I just called it Bettington. The intersection near Bettington that was growing into a small business center

also took that name. Some of these colonial houses were subsequently occupied by Peace Corps volunteers or other foreign contractors,
some by Kenyans, some used as offices, and some abandoned.

One day in 1971, a former white owner of Bettington showed up
for a visit. He had sold the house and farm to Brigadier Bettington
about a dozen years before Kenyan independence. I do not remember the man's name. He was not British, but Swiss. The man did not
stay long, just looked around and asked a few questions. Jackson did
not know him.

Jackson began his career as a houseboy and cook for a British
farmer named Baker. He later obtained his "plot" (tract, farm) of
land in Lumakanda Scheme, in part, with the help from one of his
early Peace Corps volunteer employers. Many of the Kenyan settlers
in the schemes had, like Jackson, been employees of the colonial
farmers there. They were usually referred to as "squatters."

Jackson knew several of the former colonial farmers in the area.
Except from Jackson, I heard little or nothing from other Kenyans
about the colonial past. Kenyans had moved on, it appeared. Kenya
was now their country, and it seemed of little use to dwell on or
blame the past.

The White Highlands in western Kenya, from what I heard and
read, was bush country largely unoccupied by Africans when the col-
onists came. Theodore Roosevelt toured the western part of Kenya in
1909 (Wikipedia). When Lord Delamere, the leader of the colonial
settlers, and Theodore Roosevelt reportedly sat on top of Soysambu
Rock, an outcropping located not far from the future Bettington, they
viewed wild animals as far as they could see. The rumor was that
Delamere and Roosevelt sat on the cow clipper of the Nairobi-to-
Kampala train passing through the area, shooting animals as they
went. Roosevelt, the so-called "great conservationist," killed 296
animals on his trip to East Africa for a Smithsonian collection (vox.

com/2015/7/29/9067587/theodore-roosevelt-safari). His son Kermit killed another 216 animals. Roosevelt was credited with promoting the establishment of East African wildlife reserves (Wikipedia).

In general, Jackson said little about the colonial settlers but, when I brought the subject up, he told me stories, some good and some bad. "The *waburu* (*makaburu,* or South African Boers) were the worst," he said. "They were the hardest-working people I ever saw, but they could be very rough on their African labor. For example, you needed a pass to visit the farm next door," Jackson continued. "If you were caught without one, or guilty of even minor infractions, you could be beaten, have salt put on your wounds, and then be thrown into a pit for a few days. The settlers of British descent tended to be kinder."

Jackson related a story about avoiding an attempted seduction by the daughter of a white settler. "She was a teenager and we happened to be alone," Jackson said. "She was coming on to me. I had to run away. If we had had sex and been found out, or if she had gotten pregnant, I would have been killed," he said. *"Kufa kabisa"* (dead completely), Jackson emphasized several times.

Great Britain was the first major power to officially abolish slavery in 1833, both at home and in the colonies (Wikipedia). Nonetheless, a type of "pseudo-slavery" appears to have existed on some farms in Kenya until the 1960s.

Jackson had mostly good things to say about the colonial farmers who stayed and took out Kenyan citizenship. "The good ones stayed, but the bad ones had to leave," he said. He also knew some of the white farmers who stayed on around Kitale, outside of the settlement areas. There were others around Eldoret. "We welcome the good ones," he said. "We need their expertise and still have a lot to learn. They just need to learn to treat us as equals."

In addition to keeping white judges, the Kenyan government

kept several colonial holdovers in the ministries. The Minister of Agriculture in 1970 was Bruce McKenzie from the former colonial government. I met a Kenyan ministry official many years later named "Makenzi." Never having heard of that surname in Kenya, but willing to consider it African, I asked the man where his surname came from. "I am the grandson of Bruce McKenzie," he replied. Bruce McKenzie, a promoter, and sometimes notorious wheeler-dealer whose history was shrouded in mystery, died in a plane crash near Nairobi in 1978 (Odhiambo Levin Opiyo, *Daily Nation*, June 2, 2019).

I was told by a few colonial residents who stayed in Kenya after independence that the Africans were largely "messing the place up." "You naïve Americans are wasting your time here!" I was once told by a British woman. "You don't understand this place!" This same person also told me how racist Americans were. "We don't have that problem in Britain," she said. I reflected on how unwelcome Asians were in Britain at that very time when Idi Amin was starting to evict them from Uganda. I decided not to say anything.

Later in my career, I met a Kenyan colonial son who was born in Kenya to British settlers southeast of Eldoret. Their farm was located on the equator. They constructed their house so that the equator passed through the middle of the dining room table. People sitting on one side of the table were in the northern hemisphere and on the other side of the table were in the southern hemisphere.

I got to see a dozen of the former colonial houses in the schemes. Some were used as district offices like the one in Tongaren Village, where one of the guest rooms became my office. Some houses were used as cooperative offices. Jackson, George, and I visited one house that was abandoned but had once been occupied by a previous Peace Corps volunteer. The volunteer had all visitors sign their names on one of two walls. We knew or had heard of several of the signers.

We added our names to the wall.

Jackson said that he occasionally accompanied volunteers to overnight parties in former colonial houses. Like the volunteers, he took a sleeping bag with him because there were no extra beds. He said that one morning he woke up on the floor to see a sizeable snake crawling in the rafters above him. Only Jackson's head was out of the bag. The snake fell from the rafters on top of the bag on Jackson's chest. With his arms inside the bag, Jackson flipped the snake off his chest. "I then jumped out of my sleeping bag faster than lightning!" he joked.

In Kabuyefwe Scheme one day, my agricultural assistants took me to see a colonial grave in a grassy field. The grave consisted of a flat stone on top of a vault raised off the ground. The inscription on the grave said, *"To My Wife, Hazel Ermyntrude Kilby, Who Died Here in the Flower of Her Life on 11th of July 1926. May Flowers Grow Here and No Bird or Beast Be Harmed in Hazel's Grove."* There was no longer any grove, just a tree or two.

When I visited the grave again a year later, one corner of the stone had been broken off. I decided that I should take a photo before this gravestone might be lost. My agricultural assistant and I stood for a moment in quiet reverence. I wondered about the family who had once lived there and if anyone missed or remembered Hazel. I decided that I would remember her in this book.

One oddity we encountered was a white man named Tom living on an African farm owned by Festus Wanjala in Sergoit Scheme. They specialized in pigs. We met Tom several times. He once came to Bettington to visit us. We met both men another time at the veterinary office because they needed a permit to move pigs for sale or slaughter. Tom married a Kenyan woman and took out Kenyan citizenship but had few resources to live on. In a reversed role, he became a kind of squatter employee of his African friend. Another part of this oddity was that Festus owned a legal rifle he used for hunting. Few private citizens in Kenya were permitted to own firearms.

The squatter schemes tended to have smaller plots, commonly 15 acres in size. The schemes with larger plots of more than 25 acres were more likely to have settlers from the outside "reserve" areas. Kabisi Scheme was a squatter scheme. Ndalu was a reserve settler scheme. Reserve settlers were required to have higher qualifications such as a larger down payment and perhaps a higher education.

The squatters, despite their tutelage under the colonial farmers, were usually less-progressive farmers. Kenyans told me the problem with the squatters was that they were taught to do only one thing. They were either cooks, gardeners, herdsmen, milkers, or field hands. They were seldom taught multiple skills and were not cultivated to be managers. The reserve farmers, on the other hand, had frequently managed their own small farms or other businesses in the past before moving to the schemes.

Chapter 16—Fare or Fowl?

Jackson could cook pretty much anything George and I wanted, whether English fare or Kenyan fare. We often had chicken, spaghetti or hamburger, occasional steak or fish, mashed potatoes, and green beans. Carrots, beets, tomatoes, pineapples, bananas, and other common vegetables and fruits were available in Kenya. We usually let Jackson determine the menu.

Kenyan beef was generally tough so a meat grinder was a must. Luhyas ate *ugali* all the time. It is a boiled "*mahindi*" (maize or corn) meal having the consistency of a dough. When eating *ugali,* one pulls off a handful about the size of golf ball from a communal plate, kneads it in one's hand, makes a cup out of it with the thumb, dips it into gravy or other sauce, or uses it to scoop a piece of meat or vegetable, and eats it. The most common meat I had in Kenya was *kuku* (chicken). Other foods were *nyama ya n'gombe* (beef), *nyamba ya kondoo* (lamb, the "oo" pronounced as a long "o"), and various types of *mboga* (vegetables). The most common green was *sukuma wiki* (literally translated as "push the week"), a dark green, leafy vegetable like spinach.

Large, live white termites were a delicacy for Luhyas. At the beginning of the rainy season, the termites grew wings, emerged from their underground nests, and flew to establish new colonies. Luhyas sat on the ground above the termite nests, pounded the earth with sticks or gourds to simulate thunder, and poured a little water down the holes to simulate rain. The termites emerged, and people ate the insects as they appeared. It was common to see termite wings on people's faces as they ate.

Jackson's son Kenyatta once brought a small bag of live termites from the market. George tried one and said the wings got stuck between his teeth. The nearest I ever came to eating termites was to once try them roasted with sugar. They tasted like overdone bran flakes.

Jackson fired the cast-iron stove with both wood and charcoal. It always amazed me how he could adjust pieces of burning wood or coals in the stove with his bare hands and not get burned. He did not like to handle ice cubes, however, while I could hold the cubes in my hand until they melted.

Jackson sharpened kitchen knives on a concrete or stone floor. He buffed our hardwood floors by sliding around with a piece of sheepskin under his feet. When I tried it, I almost fell on my face. "*Ni kazi, lakini si ngumu!*" (it is work, but not so hard), Jackson laughed.

Bettington, with its large yard of shrubs, flowers, and grass, was a lot of work to maintain. Although we were able to get a neighbor to come in with sheep to deal with some of the grass, we decided to hire a gardener named Simeon Simiyu. He was a Bukusu (subtribe of Luyha) from the Kitale area. Lawn mowers were virtually non-existent. Simiyu cut the grass with a long metal object having a curved blade on the end that we called a "slasher."

Simiyu worked for us for about a year. He once served as our cook when Jackson needed a break to sort out his father's finances.

I liked Simiyu and his wife Ruthie. Simiyu had a habit of stealing little things from the house, however, and, after mediation attempts with Jackson that failed to halt the stealing, we eventually let him go. Most of the objects Simiyu took we would have given him or some equivalent thereof had he asked. He was apparently too proud to ask. Simiyu returned to the Kitale area. He has since died. I have always felt remorse about what transpired.

George and I were inspired to take up chess briefly in 1972 when Bobby Fischer played Boris Spassky for the World Championship. During dinner, we sometimes tuned in on my short-wave to listen while tracing the moves on our chess board. Afterward, we played our own matches. I have not played chess since. George was better at chess than I was. I was better at squash rackets than he was.

We inevitably missed certain "simple pleasures" while in Kenya. One was good peanut butter. Kenya had its own product called Trufru. Unfortunately, the oil in Trufru always separated from the peanut part in storage. There was too much oil. I did not like the taste, either. Skippy peanut butter was apparently only available in Mombasa. So, whenever a local volunteer went there, he was obligated to bring a cache of Skippy back. It was a real treat so long as it lasted. Eventually, however, only Trufru was available. Marshmallows and chocolate chips were something we never saw either, or even remembered after a year or two.

CHAPTER 17—UP TO BATS

There were bats in the house attic. George and I did not mind the bats, knowing their importance in controlling insects like mosquitos. We seldom noticed them come and go.

A few slates on the roof came loose above my bedroom during our first rainy season. Rain came through the roof and soaked the softboard panel on the ceiling next to my bed. It sagged for a few days and then fell to the floor, just missing my bed. I cleaned it up, thinking nothing of it for the moment. The next morning when the bats came back to the attic, a few of them came down into my room, flying around and squeaking just above my head.

I would eventually replace the panel, I figured, but for the moment had to keep the bats out of my room. I found some chicken wire mesh that I tacked to the ceiling. "That will keep the bats out," I told Jackson. The next morning, three of the bats found their way down into my room through the mesh but could not fly back up into the attic. The bats dropped through the holes with their wings folded. They could not fly back up into attic through the mesh with their wings extended. I found more mesh and added two more overlapping layers, finally keeping the bats out. I fixed the roof.

Other than keeping the slates on the roof in place, we did not need to repair much. Bettington was still structurally sound while we lived there but deteriorated after we left.

CHAPTER 18—MORE
THAN A PAPER CUT

Circumcision was an important rite of passage to adulthood for young adolescent boys. Circumcisions occurred every two years in Luhya country. George, Sue, and I were invited to the circumcision of Jackson's younger brother Barasa in Lumakanda in 1971. We had to arrive at daybreak. Barasa was kept up all night, made to sit in cold river water, and splattered with mud before the procedure. To show his bravery, Barasa could not cry out. To help with his pain, he was given a stick to grasp behind his head with both hands. Another boy was circumcised also. The circumcision knife was usually kept in a special place in the house. George said the circumciser appeared to be drunk. Jackson complained later that the circumciser did not do his work very well.

Circumcisions were done in front of male family members and friends. Females stayed indoors, yet Sue was able to watch. There were often several boys circumcised at the same time. I was surprised that we were invited to take photos. I politely declined. There was dancing and drinking after the ceremony.

The boys were required to wear sack cloth, sometimes made of burlap, for 30 or 40 days afterward and to live in a separate house. "Circumcision brothers" as they were called, established a bond for life. They were obligated to help each other in times of need.

I later attended another circumcision of a Jackson relative in 1973, north of Kakamega. The procedure resulted in excessive bleeding for one of the boys. I was the only one on site with a vehicle, so I had to make a hospital run to Webuye to the north with the patient and two male relatives.

Female circumcision was illegal but still practiced in secret in many parts of Kenya. It was one of the first indigenous practices that the Christian missionaries tried to eliminate when they arrived in the early 1900s. Jackson stated that the Kalenjin tribe was more likely to be continuing the practice than the Luhyas. My African History professor at Ohio University said that female circumcision was still widespread in Africa in 1980. Ngugi wa Thiongo, a famous contemporary Kikuyu writer, indicated in his book, *A River Between,* that Christianity and female circumcision existed side by side.

Luos did not circumcise anyone, males, or females. Lack of male circumcision was a source of derision from other tribes in Kenya and, according to some, one of the reasons why Kikuyus disliked Luos.

CHAPTER 19—COLLEAGUE POTPOURRI

O ur closest Peace Corps volunteer neighbors lived just around the corner from us on the Ndalu Road. Robert "Bob" Kelly, a water engineer from our group working on the Nzoia Water Project, moved in with Larry Day, another Peace Corps water engineer who had arrived in 1968. Larry had a huge dog named Damn It. George and his new wife Sue later had two dogs at Bettington named Brutus and *Msituni* (of the forest or bush).

After Day went back to the United States, Kelly had the house to himself. Two boys approached Kelly one day with a small monkey they had captured and wanted to sell it to him as a pet. Kelly purchased the monkey. During the day, when he went to work, Kelly locked the monkey in his house. One day, the monkey discovered a cracked window and escaped. When Kelly came home, the monkey was chatting at him from a tree.

Kelly managed to recapture the monkey. The next day, he decided to lock the monkey in his kitchen when he went to work. The monkey got into the cupboards, throwing everything on the floor, breaking several cups and dishes. When Kelly returned home, he threw the monkey out.

Other water engineers from our group who lived in the area were Tim McGarry, Robert Coberly, and Robert Booth. Coberly was serving in the Peace Corps with a delayed military induction. His birthday was on September 14th, giving him the dubious distinction of having draft lottery Number 1. George and I, thanks to our program at the University of Wisconsin, both received occupational deferments from the military. The deferments gave us more flexibility to extend as volunteers if we so wished.

Having so many Roberts or Bobs around was confusing. Robert Hanchett was also in our 1970 group but assigned to a different part of Kenya. Robert Sherwood, who was living on Jackson's farm in Lumakanda, left just days before we came. However, another two Roberts came from Wisconsin in 1971. They were Robert Nusbaum, who lived in Eldoret, and Robert Haskins, who worked in Nairobi.

We were still left with four Roberts or Bobs within the general vicinity, namely Kelly, Coberly, Booth, and Nusbaum. There could have been five! My parents had intended to name me Robert, too. A Wiegand first cousin born two months before me got my name Robert before I did, so I was given my grandfather's first two names in reverse, Richard Otto. Not liking to be called Dick, I continued using my middle name and university moniker Otto in Kenya.

We solved the Robert problem. Coberly was Cob, Kelly was Kelly, and Booth was Booth. Robert Hanchett and Robert Haskins were far enough away to avoid the local confusion. As Otto, I figured I would be unique; however, it turned out that Bob Nusbaum was also called Otto. Some people knew Nusbaum as Buzz.

The chief water engineer for the Nzoia Water Project was Arthur Spore, a private contractor from California and a former Peace Corps volunteer from the first Kenya group in 1964. The project brought water from a reservoir in the Cherangani Hills more than 30 miles to the east to several of the settlement schemes in the area. A series of PVC mains and smaller lines were laid to thousands of individual farms hooked up to on-farm water tanks. The project brought clean water for household use. It functioned for several years after construction finished, but eventually fell into disrepair. I was told in 1987 when I returned to visit that there was a lack of funding to maintain the system. I also heard that the reservoir may have gone dry.

Before the water project was completed, and in situations where farmers were unable to dig boreholes due to the common bedrock in the area, women were burdened with bringing water from a river. A woman would carry a *debe* (recycled four-gallon kerosene or oil can) on her head. Sometimes she also carried a baby on her back at the same time. A ring of banana leaves on her head helped her to balance the *debe*.

Sometimes, the *debe* had a leak in one of the lower corners. The woman with the *debe* carried a tin can in one hand to catch the leaking water and then poured it back into the top of the *debe* as she walked. I once saw a woman with a *debe* with two leaks. She had two tin cans, one in each hand. I passed her by with my Moke, but her situation made me feel guilty later. "I should have offered to buy her a new *debe*," I told Jackson.

"*Shauri ya wanawake*" (that is a women's issue), he laughed.

Other volunteers from around the world working in the area included several Dutch experts based out of Eldoret. They were better paid than Peace Corps volunteers and were issued Volkswagens or Land Rovers for transport. The Dutch volunteers I interacted with the most were Huub Lamers, Jon and Hannie Wentink, Jon Werschkull, and a couple I only remember as Jaeo and Ann. Jon Mentink was called "*fupi* (short) Jon" because he was short in stature. We and the Dutch often partied together. We even climbed mountains together. Lamers played rugby with us.

We encountered an occasional VSO (Volunteer Service Organisation) volunteer from Britain. Two of them were Bernadette O'Callahan, who later married Bob Kelly, and Mary McGinnis. VSO volunteers appeared to have less funding than Peace Corps volunteers. The VSO preceded the Peace Corps, having been founded in 1958 (vsointernational.org/). We also interacted with Mieke Sacre, a German volunteer.

Unfortunately, there were two Peace Corps volunteer deaths while I served in Kenya. I met both volunteers during my first year. One was David Bogenschneider from Wisconsin, an instructor at a research farm in Western Province, who drowned in the Indian Ocean while on vacation. He was a good friend of Peter Petges. George and I knew two of his Bogenschneider cousins who graduated from the University of Wisconsin when we were there. The other death was that of Linda Manke, a nurse from Minnesota, who died in a motorcycle accident in Kisumu. Her death occurred just four days after she attended a party at Bettington.

Despite these deaths, we were always told by the Peace Corps that it was statistically safer for young Americans to be in the Peace Corps than to be back home. Traffic accidents were the biggest cause of death for people our age in both the United States and abroad. Volunteers abroad just spent much less time on the road. A VSO woman and a German Catholic priest I met also died in car accidents. The woman died in a car crash near Kapenguria, north of Kitale. The priest's car hit a train at night near Eldoret.

Besides Robert Nusbaum, the 1971 agriculture volunteers from Wisconsin included Hubert Hafs, James Orf, David Thomas, Milo Schwingle, Charles Behnke, Paul Warmka, Scott McCormick, David Jensen, Robert Haskins, Charles Magnus, and Dennis Meulemans. David Johnson, recruited in 1971, arrived in 1972 after completing a double major in engineering. There were a few other Wisconsin volunteers whose names I do not remember who worked in other programs.

Like me, Meulemans also served later as a volunteer with the Peace Corps in Paraguay. He arrived in Paraguay in the group after mine in 1977. It was quite rare that two volunteers overlapped in the same two countries. Although Meulemans and I knew each other well, neither of us had communicated with each other that we were going to Paraguay.

Several Wisconsin volunteers met for a party at Dave and Linda Thomas's house on a Sunday afternoon in Nakuru in 1972. Six of us knew how to play sheepshead, a card game originally from Germany and commonly played in only a few locations in the United States. It was mostly played in Wisconsin and Indiana (Wikipedia). Sheepshead in Wisconsin, as I knew it, was played mainly in the eastern part of the state, from Green Bay down to Kenosha or other locations throughout the state where there were German communities. Five of us played sheepshead that day in Nakuru. How many other sheepshead players were in Kenya at that moment? Although a few other Wisconsin volunteers in Kenya may have known the card game, they were not present that day in Nakuru. We were likely at a unique place in time!

CHAPTER 20—PROMISE AND TRAGEDY IN LUO LAND

W ith a nice house, a convenient location for the several volunteers in the area to meet, and a great cook on hand, Bettington became a frequent gathering place for local volunteers. On one such occasion in 1970, a volunteer nurse came up from Kisumu. She arrived in Kenya before George and me and worked in a large hospital there. Sometime during the conversation, she talked about the aftermath of the assassination of Tom Mboya.

The assassination was one of the saddest chapters in modern Kenyan history. Tom Mboya was shot by a Kikuyu gunman outside a pharmacy in Nairobi on July 5, 1969 at the age of 39 (Wikipedia). I arrived in Kenya almost a year later and remember reading about it in the newspapers on the first anniversary of his death. I knew nothing of Mboya before arriving in Kenya.

Mboya was a Member of Parliament (MP) and a Minister in the first Cabinet under President Jomo Kenyatta since Independence in 1963. He was a member of the Luo tribe, born in 1929 on Rusinga Island in Lake Victoria just off Kisumu in Nyanza Province. Mboya was brilliant and well-educated. He spent part of his youth in Nairobi, and spoke Kikuyu as well as English, Swahili, and his native Luo language. Mboya was said to have had presidential ambitions. He would have been an obvious candidate for the second or third president of Kenya. Mboya was an admirer of John Kennedy, who he visited at the White House, and was also a friend of Martin Luther King, Jr.

Mboya was shot as he emerged from the pharmacy. The alleged assassin was eventually convicted and hung. However, many in Western Kenya believed the assassin had been hired by President Kenyatta, given protection and a new identity afterwards, and that another man was executed in his place.

The assassination set off a firestorm of protest in Luo country in the city of Kisumu and in Nyanza Province. It followed on the heels of the death of another Luo politician and the first Kenyan African lawyer, Foreign Affairs Minister Argwings-Kodhek. He died in a suspicious road accident earlier in the year (globaleastafrica.org).

The Luos were in no mood for another loss. The Luo tribe, the second largest in Kenya at the time, blamed Kenyatta, and the Kikuyus for the alleged assassinations. Many Kikuyus who lived in Kisumu disappeared shortly after Mboya's death, often bound, and thrown into Lake Victoria.

A few years later, I met one of the perpetrators of the disappearances during one of my farm visits in the settlement schemes. The man was a Luhya, not a Luo. He claimed to have been living in Kisumu at the time of the Mboya assassination. He vividly described how he and his friends tied up Kikuyus and threw them into the lake to drown. "They were lucky if they drowned before the crocodiles came around," he bragged openly to several astonished listeners who were present. In any case, no one was going to turn this man in to the authorities in the aftermath. Western Kenyans were trying to put the issue aside, like other scandals or tragedies, hoping for a better future.

The man further mentioned had served with the British Army in Asia in World War II. He vividly described pursuing Japanese in Burma. "You had to be careful not to fall into a Burmese man-trap," he stated. "It was a camouflaged pit in the ground with bamboo stakes at the bottom that you would fall upon and become impaled." The man related other terrible experiences in the war. Because of his military background and actions against Kikuyus, he showed he had little fear of anyone, much less authorities.

When I related the story to Jackson about the Luhya man participating in the Luo violence, he shrugged his shoulders. "We consider Luos to be intelligent but also arrogant. Politically, we usually support them against Kikuyus."

In October of 1969, Kenyatta concluded a two-day state visit through Western Kenya to open a new Russian-built hospital in Kisumu (Wikipedia). Kenyatta's motorcade was stoned by hostile Luo onlookers. The presidential guard opened fire, killing several people. The newspapers apparently reported 11 killed. According to the nurse at our party, she saw at least 60 bodies come through her hospital, and added that there were more bodies taken to other medical facilities in the area. The event led to a two-year incarceration of the first Vice President of Kenya, Oginda Odinga, also a Luo, and the banning of his opposition political party, the Kenya People's Union.

Tom Mboya was a close friend of Barack Obama Sr., another Luo (*The Other Barack*, a book by Sally Jacobs) and the father of U.S. President Barack Obama, Jr. The last person to talk to Mboya before he entered the pharmacy was Obama Sr. The senior Obama was intelligent and competent, but also a womanizer and drinker. He held several high-level Kenya government positions but could not get along with his superiors. He died in a car crash in Kenya in 1982 at the age of 46. Mboya had been trying to get Obama, Sr. to clean up his act.

For Kenyan *Uhuru* (Independence) Day celebrations on December 12, 1970, Jackson, George, and I attended a film presentation at one of the local villages. The film was about the 1963 Independence celebrations in Nairobi, including speeches by the last British governor, and the new president of Kenya, Jomo Kenyatta. Tom Mboya, one of the founders of the new republic, was standing behind Kenyatta in the film. Instead of concentrating on the celebrations being shown in the film, the Kenyans around me kept pointing to Mboya. A woman next to me whispered "Mboya, Mboya!" I noticed tears in her eyes.

I do not like to focus on Kenya assassinations, but there were several. They were always shrouded in mystery, usually considered by the government as non-political murders at the time, never fully investigated, and then covered up. As an American who experienced three assassinations of prominent leaders in the United States in the 1960s, I was particularly sensitive to those events. I guess, in some ways, I had higher expectations for the newly independent Kenya than I had for the United States after all the turmoil of the 1960s.

I eventually visited the gravesite memorial of Mboya on Rusinga Island in 2016, relating everything I heard about Mboya to his nephew, who was on duty at the site. I also visited the Obama farm in Kogelo just north of Kisumu. I had planned to invite Jackson on these visits. Unfortunately, Jackson had died two months before.

Raila Odinga, the son of Oginga Odinga, has lost three elections for president, all highly contested. Since Independence, the Kikuyus, the largest tribe in Kenya, and the Luos, now the third-largest tribe behind the Luhyas, have been battling for national leadership. There have been three Kikuyu presidents: Jomo Kenyatta, Mwai Kibaki, and Uhuru Kenyatta; and one Kalenjin president, Daniel arap Moi.

The joke in Kenya is that how has the United States been able to elect a Luo president, Barack Obama, Jr. (a Luo descendent), but not Kenya, despite Kenya's several prominent Luo leaders and presidential attempts!

The Luos lost another prominent politician in 1990, Robert Ouko, then Foreign Minister and former head of the East African Community. Ouko was found murdered near his home outside of Kisumu (Wikipedia). The murder has never been solved but was considered another political assassination of a prominent Luo leader who could have run for president at some point.

CHAPTER 21—DEFINING DIFFERENCES, SEEKING SIMILARITIES

E arly in my experience in Western Kenya, one Kenyan asked me if all Africans (Kenyans) looked alike to me. "No," I replied. "Luos (also called Jaluo or Joluo) are usually darker and taller than Luhyas. The Maasai and Kalenjin appear to be browner." I was surprised more than once when I was trying to describe someone when the Kenyan that I was talking to said, "Oh, you mean that black man!" The longer I stayed in Kenya, the easier it was for me distinguish shades of black or brown, differences in physique, and the language sounds of various tribes.

Although Kenyans, over time, have been identifying themselves more as "Kenyan" and less as "tribal," tribes defined much of Kenyan identity in the early 1970s. There was little intermarriage between tribes. Tribal boundaries were quite distinct. Politics was tribal.

I was aware from previous studies in graduate school in 1981 of the major origins of modern East Africans, namely Bantu, Nilotic, Nilo-Hamitic, and Hamitic. Since that time, anthropologists have established new classifications. Nilotics are now Nilotes, and Hamitics are now Cushites. The Nilotes are divided into groups based on their regional origins (https://www.theafricangourmet.com/2020/05/about-kenyan-bantu-cushite-and-nilote.html). Luos are considered River Nilotes, while Turkanas, Maasai, and Samburus are Plains Nilotes, and Kalenjins, including Nandis, are Highlands Nilotes. Arabs and ancient Persians mixed with Bantus on the coast to produce Swahilis (Mijikendas). There were also small numbers of more ancient Africans, perhaps incorrectly referred to as "Stone Age," whose origins pre-dated the major groups.

The 1974 map in the front of the book shows the general location of the various tribes in Kenya. I use the term "tribe" as commonly used in the 1970s, although the proper term today is "ethnic group." The tribes with the largest percentages of the population today are Kikuyu (22%), Luhya (14%), Luo (13%), and Kalenjin (12%) (www.worldatlas.com/articles/largest-ethnic-groups-in-kenya). The Kalenjin include several subgroups such as the Nandis and Kipsigis, and roughly occupy the Rift Valley between Kitale, Nakuru, and Nanyuki, shown in green on the map, and areas to the south. The largest tribes, Kikuyu in the former Central Province, Luhyia in Western and Luo in Nyanza, live in the most densely populated areas of the country. In 2010, Kenya abandoned its provincial system, dividing its eight provinces into 47 counties roughly based on former district boundaries (Wikipedia).

Jackson often talked in terms of *kabila* (tribe) when describing Kenyans to me. He explained that Luhyas are Bantus, like Kikuyus, Kambas, Embus, Merus, Kisii, and Swahilis along the Coast. "We have some of the same words," he said. "We are also related to the Baganda in Uganda and many tribes in Tanzania and Southern Africa. However, Luhyas cannot understand the languages of Nilotic peoples, such Luos, Kalenjins, or Turkanas."

"Within Luhya, there are more than a dozen subtribes like Bukusu in this area or Kabras where I come from," Jackson continued. "We speak the same language with some minor differences. Maragolis are somewhat different," he continued. "They are Luhyas but live on the edge of Luo and Kalenjin country. It is sometimes easier for a Maragoli to communicate with us in Swahili."

One of my agriculture assistants, named Muruli, was a Maragoli. He had nine daughters and no sons. He once asked me to marry any one of his daughters, required no dowry, but just that I take her to America and give her a good home! I never met his daughters.

Being a member of a tribal community and family in Kenya, indeed in much of Sub-Saharan Africa, came with certain obligations. The concept of "extended family" was and still is quite important. It meant that close or even distant relatives were obligated to support less-fortunate members in times of need. Those with more education and higher incomes were obligated to support others who were less fortunate within the designated relational group. Elderly members without homes or resources were supported by the descendants. There were no nursing homes or government safety nets.

As the eldest of his siblings, Jackson was the arbiter, final decision-maker, and often supporter of younger siblings in need. One brother went to jail for embezzlement. Another could not seem to keep a job. Jackson was supporting two wives and, eventually, 16 children. He felt obligated to gift small items for his illegitimate children.

Luhyas, like other tribes, tended to give surnames to children based on events at the time of birth. "Barasa" was a common surname that meant the person was born on a Monday, the typical *baraza* (meeting) day. "Wafula" was a male born during the rainy season. "Nafula" was the female equivalent. "Wamalwa" was born during a time of drinking alcohol.

Many older Luhyas did not know exactly when they were born. Ages were originally counted in number of rainy seasons. Most years have two rainy seasons, one long from April to July, and one short from October to November. However, drought years, which may have occurred once every five years, could have just one or no significant rainy season. African ages could be confusing to people like me who used solar calendars.

Luhyas, like all Kenyans, typically spoke in terms of Swahili time (Arabic, Hebrew, or Middle Eastern time) when speaking in Swahili, and Western time when speaking in English. Starting from sundown to sunrise, the day begins at 1:00 Swahili time or 7:00 PM in the evening. Hours repeat in the morning with 1:00 in the morning equivalent to our 7:00 AM. The same daily time system was used when I lived in Ethiopia.

In Luhya culture, when a husband dies, his wife is passed on to one of the deceased husband's brothers, and his property is divided up among them. There are similar traditions in other tribes. Such traditions have protected widows in the past who had little or no chance to make a living on their own.

Modern Kenyan widows have been fighting this tradition for years. British and Christian influence, capitalism, and modern thought have all contributed to the change. When I lived in Kenya, a Luhya widow took the issue to court and won. She kept her property, her family, her right to live alone, and her right to remarry on her own terms if she so chose. This was the first case that I was aware of in Luyha, but I knew of a few such cases in other parts of Kenya. When I returned to Kenya for the first time in 1987, I was surprised to see so many small businesses owned by women. I rented a car from a woman-owned car rental.

I heard a story once where some Kenyan Maasai who sold several cattle and had considerable cash on hand were persuaded to deposit the cash in a bank for safekeeping. They did just that and were given a deposit receipt. However, after a few days, the elders, not really understanding banking, had some doubts about the security of their money. They returned to the bank and asked to see if the money was still there. The Maasai withdrew all the money, sat on the floor of the bank, recounted it, were satisfied that it was still all there, and then redeposited the money.

CHAPTER 22—ADVENTURES
ON THE ROAD

The 1970 agriculture volunteers were among the first to be issued four-wheeled vehicles. Extension workers like Peter Petges, who came before George and me, got motorcycles. Use of motorcycles ended in 1970 when they were deemed too dangerous. Use of Mini Mokes ended after 1974, I heard, because they were too expensive for the Peace Corps budget.

As extension volunteers, we were lucky to work during that window of a few years when Mokes were used. The Mokes greatly increased our ability to move and carry people and material within the settlement schemes. Water project volunteers were also issued Mokes. Locals would soon recognize who we were by the color of our Mokes. George's was green in color and mine was white. When Dan Dunn left after his two years, I inherited his red Moke.

George and I were not allowed to take the Mokes outside of our work or repair area. Work travel could include meetings at the provincial level. For us, that meant we could travel to Eldoret, Kitale, Bungoma or Kakamega. Bettington parties, however, did attract volunteers with Mokes from more distant places. Once there were eight Mokes in our yard, including ours.

We were not allowed to pick up any unauthorized riders other than colleagues, assistants, or farmers related to our work because such riders were not insured. I imagine the Peace Corps may also have been worried about us being robbed or hijacked. One Moke was stolen as it was parked but was later recovered.

Once on site, however, I discovered I could not pass up people who were asking for rides. I did not want to mimic the settlers before me or anyone else who might refuse to give Africans a lift. I figured, if I got nothing else accomplished on my job on a specific day, at least I was helping Kenyans do theirs. My caveat was that I would stay on my route. Most people understood this.

From the first day onward, I picked up riders, recording them, of all places, in my Peace Corps mileage book. No one in the Peace Corps ever asked for the book. I logged just over 4,000 unauthorized riders, about three per day of service. Other than being stopped once by police and ticketed 15 Ksh on a main highway for having more riders than seats, I never had a problem. I never had an accident.

George or I occasionally took Jackson to his farm, roughly 20 miles from Bettington, although he usually bicycled back and forth. On one trip, on the way back, we were stopped by police who asked to see Jackson's poll tax card. He had paid but did not have the card with him. The policeman insisted that Jackson pay the tax again or pay an additional fine. George paid the 20 Ksh. As we drove on, we picked up a young lady who waved at us for a ride. It turned out that she was looking for more than a ride. She offered to sleep with Jackson or George for 15 Ksh but said she would only charge me 10 Ksh because I was so good-looking!

Mzee Joseph Kaega, an older man who lived in Sango Scheme to the south, was a friend of Jackson's. He was later employed as a cook by George and Sue when they moved to Soy Village. Jackson got Kaega's 15-year-old daughter pregnant a year or two before George and I arrived.

One day, Kaega needed to go to a doctor in Turbo. I was asked to take him there. About halfway, a small antelope jumped out into the road, hitting the front of my car. There was no damage to the car, but the animal was dead on the spot. I do not recall if it was a *dikdik* or *duiker.* They were a rare delicacy for locals, who hunted them, even though they were illegal game. Kaega was incredibly excited to have a chance to get his hands on one of these. He begged me to keep it. "Of course, you can have it," I replied. Kaega told me that we could not keep it in the Moke because the police in Turbo might see it. So, we hid it under a tree and picked it up on the way back.

When George and I played rugby at the Eldoret Sports Club after George and Sue moved to Soy, I drove through Soy to pick them up for the games. Since George usually had a beer or two and I did not drink, I was always the designated driver, whether we took his vehicle or mine.

One night, we were coming back from Eldoret. George and Sue were dozing in the back seat of the Moke. I was approaching the railroad track south of Soy when I saw the headlights of a car that had stopped ahead. One had to be careful with trains because there were no warning lights. I thought about the priest who died when his car hit a train at night not far from this location.

However, we were not yet at the railroad tracks, but I instinctively stopped. Suddenly, there were legs crossing the road between the two cars. These were giraffes, at least three of them. I would not have seen them. My heart raced as I was just a few yards from hitting them. We could have been severely injured or killed. The roll bar and canvas top on the Moke would have been little protection from falling giraffes weighing a ton or more each. I was thankful for trusting my instincts, and especially thankful for the driver of the car in front who had obviously seen the giraffes first.

My agriculture assistants sometimes asked me to take unusual shortcuts through the settlement schemes. This was usually not a problem, except when encountering an occasional stream. Because the Moke was built so low to the ground, I sometimes had to arrange rocks or branches in the stream to stay above water or not get stuck.

There was one stream in Kiminini Scheme that I got to know well because I crossed it several times. I asked my assistant Peter Wamalwa one day why there was no small bridge there. "There was a *harambee* bridge here once," he replied. "But, after only a few days, thieves came at night, dismantled it, and took the wood. The only way to keep a bridge here would be to make it out of concrete so it could not walk away."

Having a vehicle where there were few made volunteers liable for emergency calls, especially at night. Women in difficult labor were common rides to a local hospital, usually Kitale. Bob Kelly got a few such runs. Because of his assistance, on one occasion, a newborn son was named Robert after him.

I also made a few labor runs. On one occasion, the family asked me for the name of my mother because the newborn was a girl. I was honored that the baby got my mother's name but, at the same time, I was sorry because my mother, Mildred, never liked her name. Besides, Mildred seemed an unlikely name for an African. Nonetheless, I wrote a letter to tell my mother the good news. Unfortunately, little Mildred died two weeks later.

I did not mind making legitimate emergency runs, but once refused to take a man to see a local *mganga* (shaman), telling him I would only take him to a regular doctor. Kelly took him instead. Kelly told me later that I should have taken the man because shamans were part of the African healing system. I asked Jackson later about that. Jackson answered that he did not have much faith in shamans, but that Kelly was probably right.

I was called to take a woman who had fallen off the back of a bicycle to the Kitale Hospital. She had a lot of pain in her head and neck. The 20-mile ride to Kitale on rough roads was difficult for her. A family member came along. About ten days later, I heard that she had received no medical attention at the hospital, walked to a relative's house in Kitale, and died there. Kenya's national health system had much to be desired.

The vast majority of Kenyans I encountered did not have cars, but everyone had a bicycle. The most common bicycle I saw in Kenya was the black, single-speed Raleigh. It was a real workhorse. One could see passengers on the rear carrier or handlebars. More bags of maize, cans of milk and sheets of corrugated metal were transported on bicycles in western Kenya than on trucks or cars.

I twice took Jackson's bicycle the ten miles from Bettington to Tongaren when my Moke was broken down. People stood along the road and stared. I was told when I got to Tongaren that no one had ever seen a white man on a bicycle before. Once, Jackson drove me on his bicycle a short distance to a friend's house. I was not comfortable with the idea of him driving me around so, on the way back, I drove him. Although I had considerable bicycle experience, hauling a passenger on a bicycle was not easy on local roads. Dirt roads could become like washboards when dry. Kenyans negotiated these roads on bicycles all the time and for long distances.

One day I asked Jackson to try driving the Moke. He had never driven a car before, or at least that is what he told me. He drove a mile or two on the roads around Bettington. Jackson liked it. We joked about him becoming a chauffeur for President Kenyatta!

One of the more unusual Moke requests I got was to pick up a baby's coffin from a hospital in Kamukuywa Village about 30 miles away and bring it back to a Tongaren farm. I was accompanied by two male relatives who held the coffin crosswise on their laps in the back seat. It was a sad journey, and no one spoke. Too many babies still died in rural Kenya.

When we arrived at the Tongaren farm, numerous mourners started wailing. I was totally taken aback, not being used to African funerals. I was offered money for the trip, which I refused, and was invited to stay for the funeral, which I politely declined.

"Why all the wailing?" I later asked Jackson. "We are quiet and remorseful at our funerals."

"It's the way we do it," Jackson explained.

I was told that, in previous times, large families in Kenya were necessary for labor and because so many children died. Having ten children was common when only half of them lived beyond the age of five. I heard that some families did not even name the child until they were sure it would survive.

By the 1970s, large families were still common; however, given modern medicine, more children were surviving. There was a population growth rate of more than four percent in Kenya for many years.

Kiminini Village had a police station. Twice, while living in Tongaren, I got a knock on the door in the middle of the night to help haul a rowdy drunk to the police station. Police runs always happened on holidays. The district officer should have been responsible for such trips. His excuse was that he did not have petrol in his budget to use his Land Rover for that purpose. Most often, the district officer was out of town on holidays. I got the message. After those two runs, I disappeared on holidays myself to stay with Peace Corps friends in Eldoret.

My immediate boss in the Ministry of Agriculture, James Maina, had his office in Kitale. We arranged that I would report weekly to him on Fridays. At both Bettington and later at Tongaren, locals asked me for rides to Kitale to do some shopping or other business. I usually took three riders. People approached Jackson during the week when I was out in the schemes. I often let Jackson sort out the riders for me, almost always on a first-come, first-serve basis.

Mokes were front-wheel-drive vehicles. The rear axles were small individual pieces that occasionally broke. When this happened, the suspension spring pulled the wheel against the chassis, preventing it from turning. The Moke could not move. I would be stuck out in the middle of nowhere, far from any mechanic. The trick was to take the wheel off and limp home on three wheels. This was made easier if a passenger sat on the opposite front fender to lift the rear off the ground. I sometimes had Jackson, George, or someone else sit on the fender. When alone, I looked for a large rock to prop on the fender. Once home, I was able to make the repair myself with the right tools. I decided to keep a spare axle and tools in the side compartment of the Moke for such emergencies, along with my snake-bite kit.

The petrol tank for the Moke was located on the passenger side, easily accessible for siphoning. I was not concerned about someone stealing fuel from my car. I kept a spare two-liter can and siphon tube in the car for emergencies to help other people. Several times, I met a car in the schemes that had run out of petrol. The driver would have to walk miles to get fuel or wait for another car to come along. So, if I encountered such a situation, rather than give the driver a lift to a distant service station, I siphoned out some petrol to get him to the next town. The man always offered to pay me, but I refused. "Don't worry!" I would tell him. "We fill our tanks on a U.S. government account. My government can afford to donate a few shillings worth of petrol here and there for some stranded Kenyan. It is mere pittance in comparison to the billions we are throwing away in Vietnam!"

CHAPTER 23—BROAD SPECTRUM NEWS

Kenya had a lively press, to say the least. The *East African Standard* and *Daily Nation* (*Taifa Leo* was the Swahili version) newspapers at least sounded legitimate about what they reported. President Kenyatta was considered above most criticism, but his cabinet was usually fair game. There were a lot of rumors, however, an indication to me that there were two streams of news. The newspapers had a tabloid feel about them. There was no official government newspaper, although I was sure the newspapers knew their boundaries.

With a short-wave radio, I was able to keep in touch with the world. There was Voice of America (VOA), BBC, Deutsche-Welle, Voice of Kenya, and a variety of African English-language stations that I could bring in. I occasionally listened to Radio Tanzania, Radio Malawi, Radio South Africa, and Southern Rhodesian radio. Russia and China also had programs in English.

There was a powerful English radio station that frequently featured rock music in Lorenzo-Marques in Mozambique near the South African border. Lorenzo-Marques, now Maputo, the capital, was a place where white South Africans could go on a weekend to escape the constraints of apartheid. There was legal gambling and plenty of beautiful African women.

Radio Kuwait also had an English station that played rock music. If memory serves me right, "Monster Mash" by Bobby Boris Pickett was the No.1 song on their list!

I could pick up Armed Forces Radio beamed to the U.S. Army base in Asmara, Ethiopia. They carried some live baseball and football games. I listened in on the 1971 and 1972 Major League Baseball All-Star games, starting at around 2:00 or 3:00 a.m. in Kenya. My hero, Hank Aaron, hit a homer in each of them.

Yvonne Barkley, a Liberian based in Washington, D.C., was the queen of Voice of America to Africa. VOA had a special English broadcast, done in slow English, that many Africans listened to. Many of us considered government media to be biased. I listened to BBC to get another perspective on U.S. news. My British friends listened to VOA to get another perspective on British news.

I was in Kenya during most of the Watergate scandal. As more and more revelations started to sink the Nixon presidency in 1973-74, I listened more and more to the BBC. All news tends to be sensational. I had the false impression that the United States was becoming paralyzed by the scandal.

When I returned to the United States in May of 1974, President Nixon was indeed in a lot of trouble. However, the U.S. economy just hummed along as normal. Trucks and cars were moving everywhere. Businesses were all open. The phones worked. When I called my mom from Los Angeles, she answered in a mere second or two. The country was running quite smoothly. "Who needs a president anyway?" I thought.

Chapter 24—Big Daddy, Big Problems

"*N*amna gani sasa?*" (What is going on now?), Jackson asked, when I shouted toward the kitchen one morning from another room to get his attention.

"Jackson, *kuja hapa!*" (come here), I continued. "Can you listen in on your Swahili or Luhya radio station?" I asked." It sounds like the Ugandan government has been overthrown."

I had accidently tuned in to Ugandan English-language radio on the day in January of 1971 when General Idi Amin Dada overthrew President Milton Obote in Uganda. There was martial music interrupted occasionally by someone who told everyone to stay home and remain calm. "Further news will be announced shortly," the man said. I did not know at first what I was listening to and feared at one point that something had happened in Kenya. I changed the station to find a Kenya English station reporting that there had likely been a military coup in Uganda. Jackson confirmed what I was hearing.

General Amin indeed had overthrown President Obote. Obote happened to be out of the country in Singapore on a state visit

(Wikipedia). At first, Ugandans were happy. Obote, a member of the Lango tribe in the north, was not popular with the majority Baganda tribe in the south. Amin, however, was also a member of a smaller Kakwa tribe from the north and a Muslim in a largely Christian country.

No discussion of life in East Africa in the 1970s would be complete without considering the effect of Idi Amin of Uganda. Amin's first six months in power were generally peaceful. When I spent three days in Uganda in July 1971, I felt comfortable.

However, Amin eventually expelled all Asians from the country and murdered thousands of real or imagined opponents, including intellectuals. One of his more infamously brutal murders, possibly by dismemberment, was that of Chief Justice Kiwanuka in 1972, whom Amin had appointed to that position in 1971 (Wikipedia). The rumor in western Kenya as related by Jackson to me at the time, probably inaccurate but no less gruesome, was that Kiwanuka was thrown alive to the crocodiles.

We spotted truck convoys of British soldiers traveling between Nairobi and Eldoret being sent to help Kenya maintain security on its border with Uganda. Even though many newly independent African nations were happy to see the colonial power leave, they still depended on their former lords for things like trade and security.

Ugandan refugees showed up in Kenya's urban areas. From what I remember, tourism in Kenya dropped by a third, even though Amin never directly threatened Kenya. The Peace Corps was pulled out of Uganda. Arms smuggling occurred on the border. The Pokot and Turkana tribes in Kenya near the border sometimes raided cattle from each other. When the Pokot suddenly started raiding with machine guns obtained from Uganda, the Kenyan army had to go and disarm them.

The East African Economic Community, including Kenya,

Uganda, and Tanzania, fell apart. Prior to 1971, there had been an East African Airlines, East African Railways, East African Postal Service and three national currencies (all shillings) equally pegged to the U.S. dollar at 7.14 shillings per dollar. The three-nation services all broke up, the value of the Uganda shilling plummeted, and the East African Safari Rally, a three-nation racecar event, soon became a solo Kenya event.

Although George, Jackson and I lived less than 40 miles as the crow flies from the Uganda border, we were in the countryside and several miles north of the main highway to Uganda. We were not directly affected by events in Uganda.

I met a former Peace Corps volunteer from another country who visited Uganda in 1972. He was arrested for taking a photo of a police station and detained for three days before being released. I told him that he could have easily been killed. One of the absolute dumbest things to do in any foreign country is to take a photo of a military or police installation!

A huge impact of evicting the Asians was to turn Uganda from a major sugar exporter to a net sugar importer. Jayant Madhvani (49), the head of the Madhvani Sugar Group in the Jinja area, died of a heart attack while on vacation in India in 1971 (Wikipedia). He was the head of the biggest sugar company in Uganda and said to be the richest man in East Africa. The Madhvanis left with the rest of the Asians not long after his death.

As much as the Kenya government may have despised Amin, it had to treat him carefully. Most of Kenya's electrical power came from the hydroelectric plant at the source of the White Nile in Jinja. An angry Idi Amin could have shut Kenya down.

A military force supported by the Tanzanians expelled Amin from power in 1979 and restored Obote to the Presidency (Wikipedia). Obote was a close friend of Tanzania's President Julius Nyerere.

Obote was later overthrown and removed from office again by his military. The distinction of being overthrown twice (and surviving twice) was rare, if not unique, in Africa (Julian Marshall, *The Guardian*, Oct. 12, 2005).

CHAPTER 25—EVERYONE IS DOING IT

In the tradition of many African cultures, sexual promiscuity, especially before marriage, was common practice among both young Luhya men and women. Men continued after marriage, but women would sometimes do so at their peril. During my time with Jackson, he slept around as no one I ever knew, but would not have allowed his wives to do that.

When Jackson was employed by George and me at Bettington, he kept a list of women he slept with. He admitted to me later that there were 80 on that list. Some were underaged. Several were married.

George and I often joked about Jackson being a real stud. He had quite a reputation around the area and had no problem recruiting women. Jackson just laughed at us. At Bettington, we had a neighbor who was a veterinary assistant. Out of respect for the man, who was also a devout Christian, Jackson never approached his wife. "But she asked me for sex," he laughed.

The influence of Christianity, modern medicine, western capitalism, feminism, and technology eroded many traditional African practices, especially promiscuity. More children survived. There was an increased emphasis on higher education, which could cost a lot of money. Larger numbers of children could become a financial burden. Sexual promiscuity was becoming more expensive and increasingly irresponsible. All sixteen of Jackson's children survived to adulthood.

In the 1970s, those who were sexually active had to worry about the common sexually transmitted diseases. When acquired immune deficiency syndrome (AIDS) came along in the 1980s and 1990s, promiscuity became deadly. AIDS killed many, if not most, of the prostitutes and truck drivers in Kenya. Seeing what was happening, especially in Uganda, where entire villages were wiped out, the Kenya government conducted an aggressive publicity campaign to halt the AIDS crisis.

Given the AIDS epidemic, Jackson told me on a later visit that he started using protection and curtailed his activities. He lived to be almost 77 and died of appendicitis. From what I heard later, two of his brothers died of AIDS, and one sister-in-law committed suicide after she tested positive.

I was told that Jackson's infidelity came up at his funeral. His relatives were not happy about it. One of Jackson's sons was a clergyman. Sexual practitioners like Jackson were slowly becoming a thing of the past.

Other than kidding Jackson about his sexual practices, I did not impose judgment. On the whole, Jackson was wise, responsible, hard-working, and incredibly dedicated. As indicated earlier, he was a mentor and a brother who enriched my Kenya experience. In large part because of Jackson, Kenya became like a second home for me, a priority destination throughout my life. On four of my return trips to Kenya after the Peace Corps, I gifted Jackson or his family money, usually $200 on behalf of each wife.

I have seen movies and read books portraying colonial life in

Kenya. The impression I got was that the colonial settlers were hardly the sexual Victorians they might have pretended to be. One wonders if African promiscuity rubbed off on the settlers, who were thousands of miles from the moral constraints of Europe. I also wondered at times if some of the African corruption I saw was learned from colonial settlers. Jackson told me both forces were in play.

CHAPTER 26—GARNERING
A WORLD VIEW

W hen you spend time in a new country, you get different impressions and opinions of the world and the United States. Some comments I got were accurate, many were inaccurate, but most were innocent and really made me think. The majority of Kenyans I met knew what was real and what was not about the world.

When I started doing farm visits as part of my Peace Corps extension job, at least two farmers asked me if Americans really went to the moon. I did my best to explain the moon landing that occurred just a year earlier. I recounted that I stayed up after 10:00 p.m. to watch it live on TV at our farm in Wisconsin while the rest of my family went to bed. The Kenyans I talked to believed that the moon landing had occurred but needed more information.

I heard years later that a Peace Corps volunteer in West Africa was explaining the moon landing to his Muslim students when one student said, "It could never have happened because Allah would not have allowed it." I also heard recently that someone in Spooner,

Wisconsin, where I live, considered the moon landing to be a hoax. Given the many conspiracy theories that abound in the United States today as I write, it is quite possible that a higher percentage of Kenyans than Americans currently believe that the moon landings really occurred.

One Kenyan asked me how many black people worked on our farm in Wisconsin. With 28 dairy cows, plus young stock and 120 acres, our farm was quite large by Kenyan standards. A farm that size in Kenya would have had numerous laborers. I was a bit insulted that it was assumed that white people did not or could not do their own farm work. Part of it was that Kenyans probably did not understand the extent of mechanization involved. I replied that indeed our family did all the work. We were German Americans, after all! I told the person that I never met a black person until I went to the university.

Another Kenyan asked me if I had a gun, and had I shot any Native Americans. Again, I was surprised, but understood the ignorance. Although most Kenyans I met did not have TVs, they must have been exposed somehow to American Westerns on TV or in the movies.

Kenyans were sensitive about anthropological studies that portrayed Africans as inferior. *National Geographic* photos of primitive, naked Africans were very insulting to Kenyans, I was told. I was specifically asked more than once if I was working on a masters' degree and somehow studying Africans. I assured my questioners that I was doing neither.

"Are you a spy?" was another question. I had several answers for that.

"Of course not," I said. "But, if I were a spy, I would not tell you anyway!" Then I followed with a question, "Why would a spy be working here in a remote farming area instead of hanging around Nairobi where the spy action was? Was Kenya really important enough to the United States to warrant spies?" I continued. "Besides, Peace Corps volunteers are too young and unsophisticated to be spies."

Once I was asked by a Kenyan about Black American volunteers. "Why do they seem so arrogant? Why do they act more like you and less like us?"

"Because they are Americans," I replied. "They are more likely to behave like me than you. I am sorry if they seem arrogant to you, but they are not. You will find Black Americans to be very reasonable and down to earth."

"There may be some confusion," I continued. "Black Americans are, after all, about 300-400 years separated from Africa. Many are still trying to discover their relationship with their African roots. I am also sorry if we white people seem arrogant to you. We are at least 50,000 years separated from Africa!"

Most volunteers find themselves walking in the footsteps of previous volunteers they usually never met. I was reminded more than once of how good their Swahili was compared to mine. The comparison was unfair because my critics were comparing the two-year-old Swahili of a veteran volunteer versus mine that was just a few months old.

There was one volunteer I heard about several times who had preceded me. Not only did he speak excellent Swahili, I was told, but he spoke fluent Kiluhya as well. He often walked barefoot and drank local *pombe* (beer) with the *wazee* (old men). No one could tell me, however, what his job was or if he had accomplished anything.

Kenyans often complained about the *wahindi* (Asians) to me. The Asians, originating from what was then India that included today's Pakistan and Bangladesh, were brought into East Africa in the early 1900s to work on the railroad and other colonial projects. Many Asians did not take Kenyan citizenship at Independence and were gradually transitioned out of the country. Those who took Kenya citizenship were almost always businessmen and usually quite wealthy. Asians maintained strong cultural and religious communities in Kenya, seldom intermarrying with Kenyans or whites.

"At least some of you *wazangu* will marry us Africans, but Asians never do!" one Kenyan complained to me. Asians also had a reputation as unscrupulous businessmen. Some could be aggressive and rude in business dealings, something I did not understand until I visited India after leaving Kenya. Hard bargaining, even for small transactions, was common in India.

One could assume that Kenyans knew the name of our capital city, Washington D.C., knew who our current president was, were familiar with our currency, and knew that we had been a British colony like them. I was pleasantly surprised that Kenyans who went to grade school knew about the Mississippi River and could name several U.S. states and cities. Try to test the average American on Kenya or Africa! When I was in grade school in the 1950s and 60s, Africa was still considered to be the "Dark Continent."

When I returned to the United States from Kenya and was invited to show slides of my experience, there was a lot of interest in wildlife photos. Photos of the Nairobi Hilton, streets full of cars, or Kenyans wearing suits and carrying briefcases seemed confusing to my audience.

One notices that Africa is closely tied to Europe, to the Middle East, and to the United States. Latin America was hardly ever mentioned in my four years in Kenya. When I lived in Latin America, almost nothing was ever said of Africa. Communications, trade, finance, and other important exchanges of the day flowed in the direction from Africa to Europe to North America to Latin America and back. Little moved across the South Atlantic.

When I visited Buenos Aires in 1978, an Argentinian man asked me how many languages I spoke. We were speaking Spanish to each other, of course, and he knew I spoke English. When I mentioned that I spoke Swahili, he asked, "What is that?" I responded that it was an African language used in East Africa.

"Africans do not speak languages. They only speak dialects!" he retorted. "Africans are not capable of speaking languages."

I was astounded. "But Kenya alone has 40 languages," I argued. "All those languages are fully capable of communicating the daily needs of the people using them."

The man did not accept it. "English, Spanish, Portuguese, German, French—those are languages," he continued.

"But dialects are linguistic divisions of languages, are they not?" I asked. "Spanish and Portuguese are dialects of Latin, right?" I responded with some insult. The man walked away. Perhaps dialects had a different meaning in Argentina. I knew that residents of the capital province could be arrogant. But the man clearly did not have an accurate opinion of Africa.

CHAPTER 27—HOME ON THE SCHEME

Kenyan houses were typically round, although square structures were becoming common. Where there were multiple
wives, each wife had her own house. Beds and other furniture items were lined around the wall of a round house.

There was a cooking fire in the center. This might be a pit with a
metal grate or *kijiko* (small stove). Fuel for cooking was firewood or
charcoal. The smoke traveled upward to the peak of the house where
there was a small vent with a metal covering to prevent rain from
entering. The smoke also blackened the inside of the grass roof, not
a problem because smoke acted as a kind of preservative for the roof
and discouraged any termites that might reach the roof and want to
consume the grass.

The bedding area of the house was a separate room with either
a solid wall, curtain, or sheet as a divider. Hanging on the wall of
the house was a clothes rack, a holder for a lamp, and a shelf or two.
I often saw a bird cage used for transporting a chicken, duck, or
guinea hen.

On the wall were also one or two gourds used for curing *maziwa
lala* (sleeping milk), a fermented milk product akin to buttermilk or

drinkable yoghurt. When I was first offered it, I was afraid it was not safe. But, after the first sample, I loved it. Not only was it safe, but it was good for my digestion. I am partially lactose intolerant. The *maziwa lala* was easy to digest, especially after several cups of chai earlier in the day. In addition to the bacterial culture for the drink, a taint of charcoal or ash was often part of the process, adding to the flavor. I have become a fan of smoke or ash-flavored milk, which I have now seen in several African countries.

Jackson and I later got into making a fermented milk. While whole milk was generally okay with me, I never tolerated Nido very well, the powdered milk available in Kenya.

Nothing in the Kenyan house was thrown away. Any non-usable paper was burned for fuel. Tin cans and plastic bottles were re-used. It was common for Kenyans to buy fruit drink concentrates in glass or plastic bottles. These bottles were seen everywhere and used for everything, including as candle holders.

Women did much of the work, not just in the house, but on the farm. They did the cooking, often collected the firewood, and usually went to the river or borehole to fetch water. Women did considerable gardening, hoeing of maize, and animal care. Of course, women bore most of the burden with the children, usually several in number.

Women often wore brightly colored dresses. No pants, no shorts. Even if families had little money, women tried to dress up as well as possible. Women wore their hair short, perhaps for ease of maintaining it, perhaps to avoid parasites, or probably because it was the style of the day.

I only saw one treadle sewing machine on a farm, owned by a woman who was the local 4-K (4-H equivalent) leader. All the sewing machines George and I saw in tailor shops were operated by men. Women did hand embroidery in their homes and used it as an extra source of income.

Small children typically did not wear diapers or any lower clothing until they were able to use toilets. Older children attended to grazing cattle, both on the farm or along roadsides. They carried a long stick to keep cattle in line. It always amazed me how children were able to safely control large cattle, including a bull now and then.

Chapter 28—Rhythms in Time

Like for any part of one's life, music played an important part of my Kenya memories. There were some real standouts. The Hotel Fransae in Nairobi, where we first stayed in 1970, had a restaurant and bar downstairs that constantly played "Yellow River" by Christie. George, who shared my bedroom at the hotel, complained that he was getting quite tired of the song. I just ignored it, but Yellow River leaves an indelible memory for me.

Two Nairobi volunteers had a cassette of Dionne Warwick's "Greatest Hits" that I played every time I stayed at their apartments. Warwick has remained in my Top-10 artist list ever since.

I listened to the BBC Top 40 every week on my short-wave radio. The most memorable and almost haunting song during my stay at Bettington was "Horse with No Name" by America. "You're So Vain" by Carly Simon hit the airwaves during my transition to Tongaren. Another song I distinctly remember during my transition was "Nights in White Satin" by the Moody Blues, another group on my Top-10 list.

Some songs and artists can have a disproportionate influence on one's psyche at pivotal times in one's life. Just ask war veterans.

Now, 50 years later, some music still takes me back to Kenya every time I hear it. There were also songs that were released in the United States that did not arrive in Kenya for several months. Some groups, like the Electric Light Orchestra, I never heard of until 1974 when I returned to the United States.

George had a cassette player at Bettington. He had some classical music. One favorite we listened to all the time was "New World Symphony" by Anton Dvorak.

In Kenya, we discovered African music, of course, and some of it also stuck. The Tanzanian song *Malaika* (angel) by Miriam Makeba was sung during our language training in Mombasa. I was fortunate to see Makeba in concert in Wisconsin many years later. George and Sue would name one of their daughters Malaika.

I often listened to African pop songs on the radio and discussed these with Jackson. I became a fan of so-called "African Jazz," or "Congolese" music featuring electric guitars and originating from Central or West Africa. My favorite groups were Tabora Jazz from Tanzania and Orchestral Jazz from Zaire.

Jackson and I often listened together to Kenyan ethnic music on the radio. Jackson tried to explain the nuances of Luhya music, which I kind of liked, and Luo music, which I really did not. We both loved the modern African jazz. We also discussed Western rock. Jackson was quite familiar with James Brown and Little Richard. He showed less interest in classical European music.

CHAPTER 29—HONEY OF A SITUATION

There was a crawl space above part of the living room at Bettington that was occupied by a huge nest of African bees. We could hear a hum of the bees above the ceiling panels. If we poked on the panels with a broomstick, the hum turned into a roar.

George, Jackson, and I talked several times about removing the bees, but we had no idea how to do so. The bees did not bother us. They exited outside to the backyard where there were many flowering plants that supported the bees. Nonetheless, we were fearful about getting stung or being attacked by a swarm.

African bees could be quite dangerous, not just because of their sting, but more so because of their aggression. I later got stung on my face by a single bee two separate times when I stayed with David Johnson. In both cases, one side of my face swelled up so much that I could not see out of one eye for a day. Had I been stung on my neck, without treatment, I could have died.

Jackson went to the nearby market to inquire about a solution for our Bettington bees. None of the locals would tackle the situation, he told us. But there was a certain Kikuyu man named Kamau who wanted the honey. We agreed that Kamau did not need to pay us for the honey. Removing the honey would not get rid of the bees, Jackson assured us, but it would slow them down a bit.

Kamau arrived to size up the situation. "One could probably get at the hive from the attic," we told him. We escorted him up on a pull-down ladder.

"I can come back tonight," Kamau said. "What I need are four or five *debes* (kerosene cans with the tops removed), a bunch of rolled up newspaper and a few matches. I will return your *debes* later."

Kamau came after dark. George, Jackson, Kamau and I climbed up into the attic. The first thing Kamau did was remove all his clothes. "I want to be able to flick off any bees that might crawl on me. The worst thing that can happen is to have an angry bee under one's clothing."

Kamau told us to roll up a newspaper, one at a time, and light it, creating a lot of smoke. "I need to smoke the bees to stun them and get at the honey," he said. George and I readied the newspapers as needed. Jackson handed them to Kamau. Meanwhile, Jackson held a pressure lamp, while George and I stood at a safe distance.

We watched for about an hour as Kamau reached into the crawl space to remove combs of honey. He quit when he filled the *debes*. Jackson, wearing shorts and a tee shirt, got one bee up his leg. It stung him in a most-sensitive place. He shouted and jumped around until he got the bee removed but was still uncomfortable the next few days. "No women for me for a week," he laughed. "*Nyuki nbaya sana!*" (very bad bees).

Kamau returned the next day to report that he got over 100 Ksh for the honey. Both his hands were swollen. "I'll get over that," he smiled. The bees were there for the remainder of our tenure at Bettington, but never bothered us.

CHAPTER 30—FADING GLORY

The Soy Club in Soy Village was the most exclusive hotel, restaurant, and bar in the area outside of the larger cities. There was a resident crested crane in the yard. I did not know much of its history; however, the most famous event at the club I was aware of was the visit of Princess Elizabeth in 1952. It was the second-last stop on her Kenya vacation before her father, King George VI, died in England in her absence. There is a Princess Elizabeth bedroom at the Soy Club, although Elizabeth was said by one of the owners to have slept in her train carriage instead.

From the Soy Club in 1952, Princess Elizabeth traveled to the Tree Tops Hotel in the Aberdares National Park outside of Nyeri. It was there that Princess Elizabeth signed the guest register as "Princess" and was informed the next day that she was now "Her Majesty, The Queen."

George and I occasionally treated ourselves to a fancy meal at the Soy Club, sometimes meeting with other volunteers. We once invited Jackson to come with us. A seven-course meal at the Soy Club at the time cost Ksh 15 or about $2.

The table place setting that I remember included four forks, three knives and three or four spoons. Each course, which included the main entrée, appetizer, soup, salad, cheese, fish, and dessert, demanded its own cutlery. The Kenyan waiters delivered each plate on a white cloth on their left arm and always approached to serve from the right. After each course, the waiter removed the plate and its cutlery. If we used the wrong piece, we were immediately corrected by the waiter. If we pushed a plate aside or stacked one plate on another, we were immediately corrected, if not kindly reprimanded.

On one occasion in a similar restaurant, a British guest at our table commented on what he considered rather uncivilized American table manners. "One can always tell an American because he cuts his entire steak into small pieces, puts the knife down, and then eats. The proper British way is to hold the knife in the right hand and the fork in the left, carving and eating one piece of steak at a time."

"Fair enough," I thought to myself. But when he started criticizing other American culinary habits while piling his food on the backside of his fork with his knife, I had had enough. I let him know that the Brits had something to learn when using a fork.

Jackson learned to be a cook and waiter under the British. He tried to explain proper manners to George and me, but eventually had to give up.

The Soy Club attracted many different clients, both foreign and African. One evening, we noticed an older, white gentleman sitting at another table in the restaurant. We asked the waiter if he knew who it was. He informed us that the man was John G. Williams, the author of *Birds of East Africa*, the famous birdwatchers' guide that George and several other volunteers used to note birds they had seen. I never got into birdwatching myself, being slightly colorblind and hampered by nearsightedness. I did not feel like carrying a pair of binoculars around either.

The Soy Club fell into disrepair after we left Kenya and was closed for a while. George and I met an Asian owner who was restoring and reopening the club in 2013. I briefly stood in the Queen's bedroom.

In 2016, I had the privilege of also standing in the Queen's bedroom at Tree Tops. The Tree Tops I visited was the second version of the building, the first one having been burned in the mid-1950s by the Mau Mau rebels.

CHAPTER 31—A COLONIAL CHARACTER

Our closest tie to the British past was a man named John "Jock" Rutherford. Rutherford was involved with the Eldoret Agricultural Show and other local activities. A handsome and charming man who liked to drink, he often wore a black top hat with coat for special occasions.

Rutherford lived just south of Soy Village. He managed a farm called "*Lewa* (intoxicated) Downs Estate," owned by David and Delia Craig. An estimated 200 Rothschilds giraffes lived on 3,000 acres of land located on either side of the Eldoret-Kitale Highway. It was a few of those animals that I almost hit with my Moke one night coming back with George and Sue from the Eldoret Sports Club. The farm also contained other wildlife, including kongonis, hartebeests, and colobus monkeys. Rutherford was, at one point, a manager at the Soy Club with his previous wife, Julia, and apparently stayed there at times after his divorce.

Giraffes often exist outside of game reserves. They are generally harmless, do not eat normal crops, and create quite a spectacle for onlookers. Many local farmers considered the giraffes to be a nuisance. When short of feed, giraffes could easily scale normal fences.

They took no interest in fields of maize or wheat but trampled over those crops to get to acacia trees and shrubs, their main diet.

The Kenya government eventually bought most of the Craigs' land for development. The giraffes had to go. Smaller giraffes were lassoed and sold to other private animal collectors or removed to the reserves. Some were moved to the Lord Delamere Farm in Naivasha. George helped with the roundup. Some of the adult giraffes were shot. Dozens survived in the Cherangani Hills on the Duke of Manchester's estate.

When I returned to Kenya for the first time after my Peace Corps days, in November of 1987, I learned that Rutherford had died earlier in the year. He had been staying on the coast and suffered from malaria.

CHAPTER 32—MARRIAGE KENYAN STYLE

S ue Nicolai, George's fiancée from Wisconsin, arrived in mid-1971. They were married on September 18 of that year. We lived together for over a year at Bettington.

There were two parts to the Roemer wedding: a civil service at the Office of the District Commissioner in Eldoret in the morning, and a religious ceremony at Bettington in the afternoon. Dennis Syth was the best man. Pam Chappelle, a teacher volunteer in Kapsabet, was the maid of honor. I was designated as father of the bride. As I was driving into Eldoret for the wedding, I was running a bit late and going too fast. There was a speed trap on the main highway near town. I got a speeding ticket. It was for 20 Ksh.

The man who conducted the religious ceremony at Bettington was the Reverend Joe Swick of the African Inland Mission. Foreign missionaries for the Mission were not paid well, so they had to largely earn their own way. Swick's job on the side was as a VW auto mechanic in Eldoret.

George and I first met Swick earlier in the year when we were driving to Eldoret for a meeting. Swick was stopped along the high-way. The rear engine of his VW Beetle was on fire. He was throwing dirt on it to put it out. George and I stopped to help get the fire out and then towed the car to Swick's shop.

Jackson was put in charge of the catering at Bettington. George and Sue invited 50 people to their ceremony at Bettington, but about 100 people showed up, mostly neighbors who brought children or extended families.

It was a good thing that there was plenty of food. The wedding feast included one whole cow, one sheep, one barrel of *changa'a* (lo-cal gin), eight cases of Tusker beer, eight cases of soda, two wedding cakes, and twelve gallons of German potato salad that Sue made.

In the end, Jackson asked to end the feast earlier than planned because people were putting food in their pockets and stealing some of the silverware. Jackson complained to me a lot. *"Bure kabisa"* (totally useless), he said multiple times while he, the Roemers, and I discussed what to do.

Most of the food was gone, but the potato salad, a new dish for Kenyans, was not well received. The dogs shared the left-over potato salad, according to George, but did not seem to like it either.

There were two other weddings of Peace Corps volunteers that I attended in Kenya. They were Mike Ormsby and his fiancée from Colorado, and Tim and Sue McGarry from California. I humored Ormsby, whom I had lived with during training in Mombasa, as he was smoking a last cigarette before going in for the ceremony.

Sue Roemer attended a Hindu wedding while George and I were climbing Kilimanjaro in 1973. She was invited by one of her Asian teacher colleagues from Loretto Convent in Eldoret. Sue described a part of the ceremony where the wedding party danced around a small bonfire in the middle of a dance hall, throwing grain on the fire to signify a good marriage and many children.

PART III—ON THE JOB

CHAPTER 33—DISCOVERING WHAT'S OUT THERE

I worked in eight settlement schemes north of the Nzoia River that were in Tongaren Division and part of Bungoma District. The names of my eight schemes were Soysambu, Tongaren, Kiminini, and Ndalu, located in Ndalu Location, and Naitiri, Kabuyefwe, Kamukuywa, and Kabisi, located in Naitiri Location. There were 3,500 total plots (farms). Most schemes had plot sizes ranging from 15-27 acres. There were a few special plots, larger in size, given to higher government officials. My working area covered more than 100 square miles.

George Roemer shared 11 settlement schemes with Peter Petges. Their schemes were located roughly south of the Nzoia River and part of Kakamega District. The names of George's 11 schemes were Hoey's Bridge, Nzoia, Soy, Mabusi, Sergoit, Sango, Kongoni, Lumakanda, Chekalini, Lugari, and Mautuma. There were about 5,000 total farms.

Under the Settlement Fund Trustees (SFT) agreement after independence, 66,000 Kenyan African families were settled on 1,325 large-scale European-owned farms (*Kenya's Land Re-Settlement Story*, book by P.D. Adams). I wrote a course paper on this program at Ohio University.

In my settlement area, there were two to four agricultural assistants per scheme, 25 in total. There were one or two veterinary assistants per scheme, 15 in total. The agricultural assistants worked with me under Agricultural Officer James Maina in Kitale. The veterinary assistants worked under Veterinary Officer Dr. David Baldwin at the Hoey's Bridge Settlement Office. All assistants traveled on bicycles. There were also artificial inseminators who traveled with *pikipikis* or *pikis* (motorcycles). Since there were no phones, I often arranged farm visits in advance or sought out the assistants at certain locations in the morning, usually in *chai* shops at convenient village centers.

The four schemes in Ndalu Location were politically administrated by Chief Richard Sichangi, and the four in Naitiri Location by Chief Richard Karanja. We joked about there being three Richards in administrative positions in Tongaren Division. Everyone knew me, however, as "Otto" or "*Bwana* (Mister) Otto" (pronounced oh-toh in Swahili). When I later lived in Ethiopia, in Amharic it was "*Ato* Oto" (Mister Otto, pronounced ah-toh oh-toh).

The chiefs held *barazas* (meetings) on Monday mornings once a month. Various officials reported on their work, including those in education, health, and other agencies. Beside the two chiefs in Tongaren Division, there was a district officer, two community development officers, three education officers, two home economics workers, one 4-K leader, one health officer, one police station, one agriculture extension officer (myself), and forestry or fisheries experts at the district level. I was invited to report on my work and tried to attend one of the meetings each month. Meetings were posted for 9:00 a.m., but seldom started before 11:00. "African time!" I was told. "Get used to it!"

I got along with the chiefs very well. I found them to be friendly and honest. When I asked Jackson about the chiefs, he shrugged his shoulders as usual. "I like them too," he said. "But they are African politicians, aren't they?"

My first year in agriculture extension was one of novelty and discovery. I spent considerable time doing farm visits, getting to know the territory, and getting to know my agricultural assistants. One of my assistants told me that, in the end, I would find the ten percent of the farmers who were most interested in learning and then focus on them for the remainder of my stay. Nonetheless, I needed to get an idea of what was out there.

Most middle-aged or older farmers did not speak much English or were afraid to use it. Some spoke only Kiluhya. My Swahili grew quickly. Other than greetings, I did not learn to speak Kiluhya, but was able to discern some of what I was hearing in the local language. An occasional Kiluhya word from me here and there was a good icebreaker for a conversation.

I discovered over time that farmers seem to be the same everywhere. There is a commonality of challenges and opportunities, whether it be animals, plants, prices, markets, weather, or policies. Many of the questions are the same. When I visited farms in Wisconsin later as part of my university extension job, I thought of conversations I had in Kenya, Nicaragua, and Mozambique.

Working in agricultural extension was certainly different than being a secondary school teacher. There were no set schedules, no semesters. There was no captive audience. Although there were directives from the Ministry of Agriculture, extension volunteers had to essentially invent the job. We traveled around a lot. We had to find our audience.

I visited hundreds of farms the first year. Typically, there were four or five visits a day, usually in the morning. After the usual, often repeated *mulembe mno* (Kiluhya greeting), each farmer invited me into the house after a brief farm tour. I was almost always offered two cups of *chai*. One day, there were ten farm visits, with considerably more *chai* than I needed!

Kenyans were always appreciative of my visits, even if I could not solve any of their immediate agricultural problems. I had to be careful with what I suggested because some Kenyans were almost too accepting of advice from us Americans! Most volunteers were young, barely over 20 years of age. Kenyan farmers were certainly older and had experienced considerably more of life than we had. Kenyan farmers had little financial margin for error. Whatever I suggested had to be within their context, their ability to do it, and their financial means.

The farm visits themselves were indeed special. Since the colonial period ended, many farmers had no contact with foreigners. Over *chai*, the farmers, assistants, and I spent many precious moments talking about the world and life in general. I had the overwhelming impression that most Kenyan farmers, although relatively poor and perhaps having few reasons to really like white people, would give you the shirts off their backs.

If farmers did not have *chai*, I was given bananas or a pineapple. I tried to refuse, knowing that the farmer needed the food more than I did. But my refusals were ignored. I was never short of fruit. I was getting tired of *chai*. When available, I opted for *kahawa* (coffee, usually boiled in milk). When on the road, especially in the morning, I lived on *mandazis* (triangular donuts) and *samosas* (small triangular meat or vegetable pies).

One never knows what one might discover on a farm visit. I met a Kenyan veteran of World War II who served as a clerk to a British general. He was very polite, spoke proper English, sat very straight, and had an air of importance about him. His 15 minutes of fame, so to speak, was that he witnessed the signing of the Japanese surrender in 1945 on the deck of the USS Missouri. He described his recollection of seeing General MacArthur, Admiral Halsey, and others at the ceremony.

In 1971, there was a severe drought in Kenya. The long rains, usually occurring between April and August, were sparse. There was also a serious cholera outbreak in parts of the country. Armyworms attacked several maize fields in the schemes. I later heard that 50,000 elephants may have died in the country. Whatever message I tried to bring to farmers, this being my first full year, was overshadowed by the emergency of the drought.

The second year was, in some ways, even more frustrating because, by then, I could see the problems but not many solutions. I was also homesick during my second year and suffered from a very annoying but unidentified intestinal protozoa (giardia) that eventually wore off. The prospect of being drafted for Vietnam if I returned home helped to keep me focused. I remembered my audible vow during training to stay in Kenya. I reflected on my upbringing to finish what I started.

Had I not extended for a third and part of a fourth year, my work experience would have been mostly a disappointment. It was during those years that I really started to figure out ways to get things done. My language skills were vastly improved. I developed a real liking for my host country and people. I was too young when I arrived in Kenya, not yet 22, but matured considerably by the time I turned 24.

By my third year, with the drought and frustration behind me, certain extension opportunities and priorities evolved. I was an animal husbandry officer, of course, so animal-related activities were most important. I focused on dairy nutrition, improved forages, milk quality, animal health, poultry management, and record-keeping. I taught occasional classes at the Lugari Farmers' Training Centre that was funded by Oxfam International. A nice surprise was an increasing demand for tree planting. I distributed my own version of a newsletter started by Petges called "*Ukulima*" (farming) in Swahili to about one-third of my farmers.

Ukulima was one of the more successful efforts we had in extension. Several of the subjects I covered during my time on the job included: artificial insemination, calf rearing, milk quality, dairy cattle feeding, dairy farm budgets, dairy sanitation, Desmodium legume, grass planting, cattle dipping, east coast fever, farmer's training center courses, farm measurements and calculations, foot and mouth disease, grass planting, 4-K clubs, farm shows, Nzoia water project, maize planting, mastitis prevention, farm records, Napier grass, Rhodes grass, settlement scheme statistics, soil erosion, tree planting, and even basic auto mechanics. I held two written contests for farmers based on *Ukulima* articles. Many of the articles I wrote in Swahili myself, subject to editing, of course. Several articles were submitted by agricultural assistants.

Printed material was a rare treat for farmers. They would read items several times over and never throw them away. Our *Ukulima* newsletters often got passed around to neighbors who did not receive them. George and I saw Ukulimas tacked page by page on inside walls of the mud houses.

After Dr. Baldwin took a Nairobi job, a Dr. Carlsen from Denmark became the new veterinary officer. I got to know Carlsen quite well. He had a handlebar mustache, wore safari khakis, and smoked a pipe. I once spent a night at his house in Kitale. He loved jazz, especially Count Basie and Nina Simone.

One day I received a report that a cow had died of suspected anthrax in Naitiri Scheme. I was flagged down by a veterinary assistant on my way from Tongaren to Bettington. He was not from Naitiri and had not been on the scene himself but had second-hand information from another source. The veterinary assistant added that locals were cutting up the animal for meat and carrying it away.

"*Si wezi kuwa kweli!*" (it cannot be true), I blurted out. "Are you sure?" I demanded. Anthrax did exist but was extremely rare. A case had not been seen in the area for many years. Anthrax, a zoonotic disease, not only kills animals but also people, and is highly contagious.

I had to decide what to do. I was halfway between Naitiri and the vet office, about 15 miles either way. If I went back to Naitiri, what could I do? I was no expert on the disease. I was not sure what I would do when I got there or what I would find. I would waste precious time. It was late in the afternoon. The veterinary officer might soon go home to Kitale. Of course, there were no phones!

I drove hurriedly to the veterinary office. Carlsen was still there. He jumped out of his chair. "What?" he shouted. Carlsen did not believe it. All I could tell him was what I heard.

"Go to the Naitiri village center and find one of your assistants," I told him. Although I would have gone along, Carlsen dashed out to his Land Rover and sped away. Thankfully, it turned out to be a false alarm.

Most of the plowing on scheme farms was done with oxen. Tractor plowing was becoming more common as farmers could afford it. An occasional farmer had his own tractor. However, custom operators, usually Asians or wealthy Africans, circulated with their tractor-plow crews in the dry season before the rains began. The plows were disk plows, not moldboard plows. Two operations were usually necessary to prepare the soil for planting.

I stopped to view one such plowing operation. The Asian owner, who had Africans driving his two clutch-driven, Massey-Ferguson tractors, asked me if I had ever driven a tractor. "Sure," I replied. "I grew up on a dairy farm. I have been driving tractors since I was seven."

The Asian signaled one of his drivers to stop. "Have at it!" he said, pointing at the tractor. "Third gear." I made two rounds.

There were no work horses of any kind in the settlement schemes. In fact, George and I saw no horses on farms at all. Horses were expensive to keep and less resistant to local conditions than oxen. The British kept riding horses often used for dressage and other sports competitions. We saw them at agricultural shows. It could be said that Kenya missed a potential generation of draft power used in Western nations, skipping horses, and moving directly from oxen to tractors. Kenya, like much of the developing world, also largely skipped land-line telephones in rural areas, moving from post office mail and other physical messaging directly to cell phones.

I read that horses do not survive in many parts of Africa because they are particularly vulnerable to "*nagana*" (trypanosomiasis or sleeping sickness) spread by tsetse flies. The flies were not common on the cultivated East African plain, but more of a nuisance in the humid tropical forest and shrub environments. I do not remember any encounters with tsetse flies in western Kenya, but later saw many of the flies in forested parts of western Ethiopia.

We also saw no donkeys in the settlement schemes either. We saw one or two at agricultural shows. Where I saw increasing numbers of donkeys over time was in the outskirts of Nairobi. Donkeys are certainly cheap and efficient forms of transport labor. Nonetheless, I was perplexed by that, because I expected to see more small, motorized vehicles doing similar work closer to Nairobi. Donkeys, along with camels, are the most common beasts of burden in Africa. Camels are found in northern Kenya.

The principal companion animals in the settlements were common dogs and cats. They were often not well-cared for, appearing thin and mangy. When I mentioned that pet dogs and cats in the United States might live indoors and sleep with their owners in bed, local Kenyans laughed at or scorned the idea.

In 1972, the Kenya government decided to transfer all extension in the settlement schemes from the Ministry of Agriculture to the Ministry of Lands and Settlement. There were no changes in staff at our level; however, George and I, in addition to our regular reporting, now had to report to the area settlement controller in Eldoret.

In Africa and many parts of the world developed under European systems, extension was an arm of the Ministry of Agriculture. Agricultural research was usually a separate institution under the ministry. Neither extension nor research were part of the university system. In the United States, agricultural extension and research are often, if not usually, part of a university. I prefer the U.S. system because I have often found a disconnect in Africa between education, research, and extension.

The area settlement controller in Eldoret was a Kikuyu fellow. Western Kenyans could be resentful of having Kikuyus in high positions on their turf. As usual, I asked Jackson for his opinion. "Whatever you may dislike about their politics, Kikuyus are more likely to get things done," Jackson replied. I liked the man. He was very conscientious, with a lot of responsibility on his plate.

One day, the controller confided to me that he had a teen-aged daughter with epilepsy. He wanted to get her to the United States for better diagnosis and treatment. He was not rich but was willing to spend some money to get her there. I offered to contact one of the larger medical centers in New York on his behalf. I wrote what I thought was a passionate and reasonable letter, but I never got a response. After several months, I apologized to the controller, feeling quite disappointed.

CHAPTER 34—BETTER RUMINATION

Settlement farmers were issued improved "grade" dairy cattle as part of the SFT loan agreement. Grade cattle largely included Friesians, Jerseys, Ayrshires, Guernseys, and Shorthorns. These breeds gave a lot more milk than the native *zebu* cattle breeds (Boran and Sahiwal), but were less resistant to local challenges like tick-borne diseases, internal parasites, poor forages, drought, and hot weather. By the time George and I arrived, about half of the farms no longer had any grade cattle left, just native cattle. We often complained to our assistants about all the *shenzi ng'ombe* (lousy cattle) we were seeing.

Improved forages were extremely important. They were higher yielding and more digestible than native forages. These included pasture grasses such as Nandi Setaria, Rhodes, Star, and Kikuyu, and legumes such as Greenleaf and Silverleaf Desmodium. Elephant or Napier grass and sometimes sorghum were the common cut-and-carry forages. I bought bags of forage seeds from the Kenya Seed Company, conveniently located for me in Kitale, and sold them to farmers and cooperatives.

George and I got at least 50 farmers to establish improved forage plots. We scheduled field days (pasture walks) open to the public. Improved forages were one of the success areas we had in extension. On visits 20 years later to my former schemes, I was happy to observe that many farms succeeded with their forages and grade cows.

Maize (corn) silage was a great forage if farmers knew how to make it. However, the idea was still new on the schemes. Making silage involved extra labor and equipment. The process involved chopping the maize grain together with the stalk. Many Kenyans, indeed, many Africans, objected to the idea of feeding maize grain to animals when so many people on the continent were hungry.

One farmer overpopulated his maize when planting, so he told us we could try to make silage from the thinned-out plants. The farmer dug a pit under a small milking shed roof. Laborers cut maize stalks with *pangas* (machetes) and brought bundles to the shed. Three of us chopped the stalks by hand with machetes on small kitchen tables covered with planks. We dumped the chopped maize into the pit, adding molasses to enhance fermentation. After filling the pit with about two tons of silage, we stamped on the silage to compact it and covered it with dirt.

The farmer opened the pit after a month, as instructed. His cattle did not eat the silage. It was too sour. Our mistake was that we harvested the maize too early at an immature stage. Even with molasses, the extent of fermentation was not enough to produce good silage. Maize silage needs to be made when both the full cob is included, and the plant is mature enough to contain considerable levels of carbohydrate.

I learned later that a South African farmer near Eldoret was making a bunker silo for maize silage. George and I talked to him at the Eldoret Sports Club. When I returned to Kenya in 2016 on a Farmer-to-Farmer dairy project in Nandi, a Kalenjin area, I found that more than half of the smallholder farmers there were successfully making maize silage in pits or bunkers.

Dennis Syth promoted silage-making in his work area in Central Province. It was Napier grass silage, however, because maize was still considered human food, not animal feed. The main Kikuyu diet was maize grain and beans. When I fed maize grain to sheep in one of my feeding trials in Ethiopia in 1990 for graduate research, I was criticized. "People are hungry." I was told. "Maize is for humans, not animals."

I learned about a drought in Kenya in the 1960s when the U.S. government donated tons of maize grain to Kenya for food. Western Kenyans hated it. It was yellow maize (field corn) as opposed to the common white maize in Africa. Kenyans told me that it was difficult to make *ugali* from it and they did not like the taste.

One of my regrets was that I totally missed the importance of the tropical tree legumes that grew in the area. I realized this when I later focused on them for my graduate studies. My PhD forage tree was *Sesbania sesban,* which grows all over East Africa and the Middle East. I eventually became something of a world expert on the tree and its nutritional qualities. I saw Sesbania in Jackson's backyard when I visited Jackson's farm in the 1990s. "That's goat plant," Jackson said. I suddenly recognized Sesbania everywhere, even in Serengeti when I returned there in 2006.

Rotational or managed grazing was another area that could have greatly benefited Kenyan farmers in the 1970s, but I was not aware of the concept at the time. I first saw the practice in South America in the late 1970s, and it was not until the 1990s that Wisconsin farmers started to seriously adopt it. I coordinated a grazing network for extension in Wisconsin in the 2000s. When I returned to Kenya on a dairy project in 2016, I found some Kenyans practicing managed grazing and felt quite competent to promote the practice.

CHAPTER 35—MINIMIZING THE BULL

I conducted agricultural surveys of my settlement schemes in the latter months of 1972, and again in 1973. Data collected included animal populations and practices. The data were supplied to me by my agricultural and veterinary assistants. Much of what was reported were estimates; hence, there never was any great promise of accuracy. However, the statistics gave me a snapshot of what was going on in the schemes. The results were incorporated into reports submitted to colleagues and up the chain of command to the minister himself. My boss, James Maina, appreciated the reports, as did my agriculture assistants. I received no response from the Ministers of Lands and Settlement or Agriculture for either survey.

Artificial insemination is the most efficient and inexpensive way to improve the genetics of a dairy herd. According to my survey for 1973, 66% of settlement scheme famers were using artificial insemination for their cattle, covering 35% of serviceable animals. Not all cows conceived on a first attempt, however. Assuming only a 50% first service conception rate, the number of serviceable animals would be considerably lower. That meant that bulls were used for most of the conceptions. Keeping bulls was expensive and dangerous. Too many of the bulls were *zebus*, slowing down or reversing genetic improvement for milk production.

Inseminators did not come to the individual farm, but kept a regular schedule at a "crush," a central location, usually at a cattle dip, where farmers could bring their cows. Herding cows to the crush every time they were in heat was an inconvenience for many farmers.

There were the usual complaints by farmers about the artificial insemination service, including that inseminators would sometimes not show up, or that the wrong semen might be used. The service cost of 10 Ksh per insemination was too high for many farmers who could get the service of a local bull for 5 Ksh or with an in-kind payment of a chicken.

Responding to those complaints about cost, President Kenyatta himself issued a directive to lower the price to 1 Ksh. The cost difference was to be subsidized by the federal government. Whatever the price and whatever the problems, Kenya overall had a substantial and effective artificial insemination service that it could be proud of.

When I was consulting with the African Development Bank several years later as part of an artificial insemination project in Uganda, I asked my hosts there how many inseminations had been recorded in the past year. "Over 18,000," I was told. The man was rather proud of that number.

I then asked if he knew how many Kenya recorded in the same year. "About 400,000," he replied. I have not been able to substantiate those numbers.

Kenya is about twice the size of Uganda and has about twice as many people. However, the percent of arable land in Uganda is roughly 34% while in Kenya it is only about 10% (World Bank Data). Uganda, a beautiful green country with considerable water resources, suffered through Idi Amin, a subsequent civil war, and a devastating outbreak of AIDS. Kenya, on the other hand, became

the economic powerhouse of East Africa. Counting artificial inseminations of cattle, in my opinion, was just another way to compare
economies.

CHAPTER 36—IMMERSION FOR LIFE

The settlement scheme cooperatives were assigned the duty of maintaining the cattle dips in the area. Plunge or immersion dips were the main device for killing ticks on cattle. Dipping was done once a week.

A dip was a concrete structure with wooden sides and a roof, about 20 feet in length, 10 feet deep at the entrance, and just a bit wider than a cow. It was filled with water mixed with a few gallons of an acaricide for killing ticks. Cows and youngstock were led into a corral that funneled toward the dip entrance. Animals jumped into the dip, swam its length, and then walked up a ramp on the exit end. In the process, animals were completely covered with water containing acaricide. A man with a brush at the exit cleaned the ears and under the tailheads of the animals where there may have been air pockets. All cooperatives that I worked with used plunge dips.

Blue and red ticks spread several cattle diseases, including anaplasmosis, heartwater, tick fever, and East Coast fever. There was no treatment for East Coast fever at the time, and mortality was 100%. Ticks also caused wounds and blood loss, predisposing cattle to other ailments.

East Coast fever killed many dairy cattle. The grade breeds that farmers wanted to propagate for increased milk production were especially vulnerable. Indigenous *zebus*, on the other hand, were largely resistant to tick-borne diseases. Tick-borne diseases wiped out many of those grade animals that were not vigilantly dipped.

The acaricides, the active chemicals used against ticks in the dips at the time, were organochlorides and organophosphates. Arsenic had been used for decades in many tropical countries until ticks became resistant to it. Ticks were becoming resistant to organochlorides when I was in Kenya, so organophosphates were increasingly being used. The veterinarians and industry representatives I talked to were pessimistic about the future after organophosphates. "There is nothing new on the horizon to fight ticks," they said.

Poor management of the dips was a huge threat. If cooperatives did not keep the acaricide at the proper level, tick resistance could occur. If dips were not cleaned out regularly, dirt, manure, and other debris would render acaricides weak or useless, further increasing tick resistance.

I did not know the extent of dip mismanagement but saw that many grade cattle died. Several farmers purchased hand-spraying equipment and treated their own cattle at home. Dips were supposed to be tested regularly. I was not sure how well that was done.

CHAPTER 37—SHOWING THEIR STUFF

Agricultural staff members were required to participate in the local Agriculture Society of Kenya (ASK) shows. I worked at the agriculture booth in Kitale, and George worked at the one in Eldoret. Just for fun, I entered a chicken as an exhibit at one of the shows. It was the only entry in its class, and I won first prize. First prize in Kenya garners a red ribbon, second prize a blue, and third prize a yellow.

George and I attended the show in Kakamega. I took a couple of my assistants along. One vendor sold ice cream cones. It marked the first time I had seen ice cream outside of Nairobi. I bought cones for my assistants. They had never seen ice cream before. One of them complained that the ice cream made his teeth hurt, perhaps because he may have had tooth decay.

One day at the Kitale Show, a young man of secondary school age came by. He asked me a barrage of questions about cattle nutrition and other subjects that were much above my level of understanding. I did not know how to answer him. He left in frustration. My assistant, who had met him before, told me that the fellow was obviously a genius. "There is always a small percentage of such people in every population," he told me. The assistant hoped the young man would find his way into college and use his abilities to the fullest. "Too many intelligent young Africans get lost along the way," he mused.

Some of the more interesting booths found at all the shows were those of the Kenya Prison Industries. Prisoners created several types of traditional crafts and curio items that were sold to Kenyans and tourists.

George and I attended the ASK Show in Nairobi. It was a large show that included tribal dancers and British horsemen. It was there that we saw President Kenyatta and Vice President Moi. Kenyatta gave his famous *harambee* speech, waving his ornate fly whisk. *Harambee* was Kenyatta's theme for nation-building. We took photos, from a distance, of course. If *askaris* (soldiers, police) caught anyone taking a photo of the president, they would smash or confiscate the camera.

George also attended the Kamariny Show east of Eldoret on the edge of the Rift Valley. It was in Bob "Otto" Nusbaum's working area. George recalled meeting a poorly dressed, older Kenyan who produced from his pocket a collection of drivers' licenses from Europe. The man had been a driver for British generals in Europe during World War II.

The Kamariny Show was famous for its tribal dancers who came in from far and wide. Unlike other shows around the country, the female dancers there did not wear tops.

CHAPTER 38—PROMOTING CHACHA

One of my agricultural assistants in Tongaren Scheme was Anthony Chacha Omari, known as "Chacha." Most of my assistants were three-year agricultural graduates of technical colleges. Egerton College near Nakuru was one of the more famous ones, and another was Embu. Chacha was unusual in that he had the equivalent of a bachelor's degree from the Soviet Union. He spoke fluent Russian. Chacha was from the Kuria tribe south of Kisii on the southwest border of Tanzania. About two-thirds of the Kurias lived in Tanzania (Wikipedia).

Chacha was one of several students from southwestern Kenya given scholarships to study in the Soviet Union or other Eastern Bloc countries by the leftist Vice-President Oginga Odinga, a member of the Luo tribe. Many of those scholarship recipients were Luos.

One Luo who studied abroad on a scholarship in 1961, before Kenyan independence and before Odinga's scholarships, going to the United States instead, was Barack Obama, Sr. His scholarship was arranged through a program organized by Tom Mboya (Wikipedia).

By the time Chacha and others returned, Odinga was out of favor with the Kenya government and out of power. The Eastern Bloc graduates who worked for government were not given good positions. Chacha was clearly over-qualified and certainly underpaid for his abilities. He and I became good friends.

Chacha asked me one day if he could join the Peace Corps. I replied that only American citizens could join the Peace Corps. However, the United Nations had a new volunteer program modeled after the Peace Corps. I found the address and suggested that Chacha apply. He did and was accepted for assignment in North Yemen.

I kept in touch with Chacha. When I left Kenya in 1974, I passed through North Yemen, spending a week with him there. When his assignment ended, Chacha joined the Food and Agriculture Organization (FAO) in North Yemen. When I returned to Kenya in 1996 on an African Development Bank project, I heard that Chacha had retired and was living in Nairobi. I was proud that I was able to help him get out of his situation and move up in the world.

CHAPTER 39—COOPERATING KENYAN STYLE

Each settlement scheme had a government-mandated farmer cooperative. Farmers were required to be members of their scheme cooperative and to use that cooperative for certain activities. Cooperatives were charged with collecting milk, destined for the Kenya Cooperative Creameries (KCC), and collecting maize destined for the Kenya Maize and Produce Board. Cooperatives were also charged with managing dips for treatment of ticks for livestock. Cooperatives sometimes provided products and services like seeds, veterinary drugs, and trucking.

Cooperatives collected loan payments on land. Farmers who were not making good use of their land could be threatened with eviction. They would be told bluntly that there were plenty of people who needed land and would be happy to take their farm. I was on one such farm having only a half-acre of crops during an encounter with visiting Kenyan officials. The farmer, a rather defiant fellow, basically said that his job was to sit in his chair and tell family members what to do. I never heard of anyone being evicted. Some farmers attempted to buy several plots. Initially, that was not allowed.

A plot of land, once in the family, would usually stay in the family. Land was passed from generation to generation. People were buried on their land. There were no cemeteries in rural areas. Land was often subdivided among sons. There was a special permanence about a piece of land. Even those who moved to the city always had a plot somewhere in their home area.

To my knowledge, there were no other legal market outlets for scheme milk and maize for cooperative members. Some farmers were not cooperative members, however. It was never clear to me if they were legally allowed to sell to the private market or there was some other reason. Some farms may have lost their cows to tick diseases or did not produce enough maize to sell.

Even though I did not work directly with the cooperatives, they could be a huge headache for me. Cooperatives were often behind on payments to farmers, so my efforts to get farmers to invest in improvements on their farms were constantly stalled by lack of cash and frustration. Payments for maize delivered to cooperatives in December were often not received by farmers before the next crop planting in April.

Cooperative chairmen and other officers were sometimes corrupt or incompetent. Rumors were common that funds were mismanaged or embezzled. Services promised were sometimes not delivered or only delivered to favored friends or relatives. Farmers complained to me constantly. Even Jackson's brother, who worked for a cooperative, was charged in a land scandal and went to jail. At least there was some enforcement of law.

Dan Dunn, Dennis Syth, George Roemer, and Otto Wiegand
Philadelphia, Pennsylvania–1970
Courtesy of George Roemer

Otto Wiegand and Dave Wieckert–Madison, Wisconsin–2017

Mombasa Entrance–1970
Courtesy of George Roemer

Peace Corps Training–Mombasa–1970

Otto Wiegand's Mini Moke–Bettington–1970

Jackson Sikolia and Simeon Simiyu–Bettington–1971

Jackson Sikolia and Alan Johnston—Soy Scheme—1969
Courtesy of Alan Johnston

Jackson Sikolia with Parents, Baby Sister Alice, Sons: Kenyatta, Richard
Lumakanda Scheme—1970
Courtesy of Alan Johnston

Jackson Sikolia and Joseph Khaega–Soy Scheme–1970
Courtesy of Alan Johnston

Jackson Sikolia and Friend–Soy Scheme–1969
Courtesy of Alan Johnston

Round House on Jackson Sikolia Farm–Lumakanda Scheme–1970

Square House on Jackson Sikolia Farm with View of
Uganda Highway–Lumakanda Scheme–2013

Peter Petges and Friend Holland–Kamariny Show–1971
Courtesy of George Roemer

(Left to right) Colleen McGarry, Sue Roemer, George Roemer, Tim McGarry, Sue McGarry, Bob Booth, Bob "Cob" Coberly, Bernadette O'Callahan, Otto Wiegand, Bob Kelly, Dave Johnson, and Joe Berquist–Tambach–1972

Sue Roemer–Lewa Downs Estate–Hoey's Bridge–1972
Courtesy of George Roemer

Otto Wiegand–Mount Kenya–1971

Jim Orf, Bob Nusbaum, Dave Johnson, George Roemer, Porter, and
Otto Wiegand–Mount Kilimanjaro –1973
Courtesy of George Roemer

Mount Kilimanjaro from Amboseli Park–1972
Courtesy of George Roemer

Sally Johnston with Jackson Sikolia on Soysambu Rock—1970
Courtesy of Alan Johnston

Mount Elgon from Soysambu Rock—1971
Courtesy of George Roemer

George and Sue Roemer, Dennis Syth, and
Pam Chapelle—Roemer Wedding—Eldoret—1971

Tina, David, Jackson Sikolia, Richard, Kenyatta, and
Angela—Roemer Wedding—Bettington—1971

Lee Swan, Agriculture Assistant, and
Farmer Joseph Makokha–Kabisi Scheme–1971

Otto Wiegand at Work–Tongaren Scheme–1971
Courtesy of David Wieckert

Farmstead Scene–Kiminini Scheme–1973

Improved Pasture–Kiminini Scheme–1973

Cattle Dip–End View–Lumakanda Scheme–1972
Courtesy of George Roemer

Cattle Dip–Side View–Lumakanda Scheme–1972
Courtesy of George Roemer

Peter Wamalwa (in red) and Friends Drinking Busaa–Kabuyefwe Scheme–1970

Primary School–Soysambu Scheme–1971

Peter Petges's house near Jackson Sikolia Farm–Lumakanda Scheme–1970
Courtesy of Alan Johnston

Otto Wiegand and Mud House–Tongaren Village–1973

Colonial Grave–Kabuyefwe Scheme–1971

Jock Rutherford–Eldoret Show–1973
Courtesy of George Roemer

Clementina, Angela, and Tina at Jackson Sikolia Grave
Lumakanda Scheme–2016

Jackson Sikolia Grave–Lumakanda Scheme–2016

Nairobi–1970

Otto Wiegand–Nairobi–2013

Alan Johnston During Filming of Out of Africa–Nairobi–1985
Courtesy of Alan Johnston

Otto Wiegand and George Roemer at
Karen Dinesen House–Karen, Nairobi–2013

CHAPTER 40—CASH COW

The price for maize set by the Maize and Produce Board—30-40 Ksh per 50 kg bag, as I recall—was often lower than the black-market price. Farmers were permitted to keep a portion of maize for family use. But they generally under-reported yields, often delivered only a fraction of their maize to the cooperative, and then sold the rest on the black market for a higher price.

The milk price of 3.50 Ksh per liter, also set by the government was, on the other hand, quite good. I calculated that it was better than the price received by dairy farmers in Wisconsin at the time. I told my farmers to increase milk production by growing more improved forages and to pay less attention to maize. Kalenjin farmers to the south and east, good cattle people according to my Peace Corps friends who worked in those areas, seemed to have the milk idea figured out. Luhya farmers, in my opinion, were still too focused on growing maize.

Cooperative milk collection centers, where most of the milk was delivered, could be a sore point. Collection centers were typically small, grass-roofed canopies. Farmers arrived with one or two small containers of milk, usually a few gallons each, strapped to the back of a bicycle. A cooperative employee charged with weighing each farmer's delivery did the so-called "smell test" before co-mingling milk. This test was essentially a visual observation for dirt, and thick milk, an evidence of mastitis. Tests for added water or bacteria, conducted at the plant, were not available at collection points. A dishonest employee sometimes accepted milk from relatives or friends that should have been rejected. Co-mingling the bad milk with the good downgraded the whole lot. Farmers complained to me that they often did not get the money they deserved for their milk. Some farmers found ways to get around the rules. Some who had access to their own daily transport for milk found ways to get direct contracts with the Kenya Cooperative Creameries (KCC).

When cooperatives worked well, they could be an incredible advantage for farmers. Sergoit Cooperative was a notable success story. It had a milk can cooler for evening milk. The cooler was a pit in the floor where cans of milk were stored with cold water circulating through the pit. I learned after I left that Ndalu and several other cooperatives had installed coolers.

Coolers enabled famers to deliver evening milk as well as morning milk. Only morning milk was collected by the KCC contract transporter. Because of that, farmers milked their cows on 16:8-hour schedule to put more milk on the truck in the morning and keep less milk in the evening for their home use. Being able to sell and deliver evening milk to the cooperative allowed farmers to milk on a 12:12 schedule, better for the comfort of the cow and likely to result in more milk from the cow.

The Sergoit Cooperative once ordered hundreds of bags of Nandi Setaria, an improved pasture grass seed, for their members to plant. Sergoit functioned well, in large part, because it had a treasurer named Shafan Lunani. Lunani, a man in his 60s, had no reason to be tempted by corruption at the cooperative because he was a self-made millionaire.

Lunani owned the general store and petrol station in Turbo. I was told that he owned or invested in a sugar mill in the Kakamega area. From what Jackson said, Lunani did not have much education, yet spoke good English. Despite his status, Lunani often waited on customers himself in his general store, including George and me. Shy to expose his English, he only used Swahili with us. Jackson always spoke of Lunani in glowing terms. Lunani was not just a Luhya; it turns out he was also a Kabrasi from Jackson's home area.

Among my scheme cooperatives, the Ndalu was the best one. Ndalu had the best-educated and wealthiest farmers. The cooperative built a new warehouse and offices. It owned a lorry (large truck) that could be rented for members to haul crops, building materials, or equipment. Even so, there were still complaints that the lorry was usually kept at the chairman's farm, and that cooperative services were discounted or free of charge for cooperative officials.

CHAPTER 41—FIRING THE MILKMAN

Rift Valley Transport sent out numerous milk lorries before sunrise every day to pick up milk from cooperatives and milk collection centers in western Kenya. The trucks took their loads of cans to Kenya Cooperative Creamery (KCC) processing plants in Eldoret, Kitale and other locations. Typically, trucks started their routes at 4:00-5:00 a.m. and delivered their loads sometime around midday, if not before.

There were problems. The trucks were not refrigerated. They often had no canvas or other cover over the cans to protect them from the heat of the sun. Drivers were paid overtime after eight hours, so staying out later gave them extra pay, exposing the milk cans to even more sun. Drivers could be seen at bars over lunch time with loads not yet delivered.

At first, cans were labeled, of course, but not sealed. A dishonest driver might bring his own empty cans or top up those of his friends or relatives with milk from other cans. After stealing milk, the driver might add water to the other cans. I saw one milk truck driver adding water to cans from a dirty waterhole.

At more than one meeting with the area settlement controller, we brought up the issue of the milk transport. I mentioned seeing the trucker taking water out of a mud hole. Other settlement officials in the meeting were also aware of the problem. Rift Valley Transport, the only milk hauler in the region, had no authorized competition. The company was owned by Vice President Daniel arap Moi.

It was decided during one meeting that a letter must be written to the Minister of Lands and Settlement and to Vice President Moi himself. George and I sensed quite quickly that no one in the room was brave enough to write such a letter. Even the area settlement controller, who could have done so with considerable authority, probably feared for his job.

George and I were asked to write the letter. We were surprised. Our response was that we were temporary, just Peace Corps volunteers, and that Kenyans should have to solve this issue on their own.

News of the problem must have gotten up the administrative ladder somehow. The Minister of Lands and Settlement, Masinde Muliro, a western Kenya Luhya, suddenly owned a milk transport system operating in the region. There was no problem for about a year. Then I heard his drivers were guilty of the same abuses.

CHAPTER 42—BIG CITY WEST

Eldoret in Rift Valley Province, with a population of 20,000, was one of the largest cities in Kenya when I arrived in 1970. By comparison, Nairobi had about 500,000 people at that time. In Eldoret, one could walk from one end of the city to the other in about 20 minutes. Today, Eldoret is the third largest city in Kenya at 400,000, behind Nairobi at 4.7 million and Mombasa at 1.3 million (MacroTrends.net).

The growth of Eldoret had much to do with its location as a major hub to the west and northwest. When Daniel arap Moi, a Kalenjin from the area, became vice president and then the second president, he invested heavily in Eldoret and the surrounding Uasin Gishu District. A new university called "Moi University" was established. I visited it in 1987.

Eldoret still has a clock tower in the center of the city. There were three main streets when I was there: Kenyatta, Oloo, and Oginga Odinga, that went down the hill from the main highway toward a river. These three streets were designed in colonial times to be wide enough to turn a six-oxen team and wagon around. Most of the commerce in the early 1970s was on the main highway or those three main side streets.

Eldoret had the only supermarket in the area. It was called Hassanalis. I only went there once or twice. After getting used to buying my essentials in small *dukas* (shops) or at roadside stands, a supermarket seemed strangely out of place in my life.

Eldoret had two British banks: Barclays and Standard. Given the sizeable Asian community there, I maybe expected to see a Bank of India like the one in Nairobi, but there was none. I often ate fish and chips at a small Asian restaurant called Sparks Milk Bar. A Sikh named Sagoo repaired my Moke. Another Asian called Sultan also fixed cars.

Dan Dunn rented a house from a Mrs. Obura on Kisumu Road, past the river up toward the Eldoret Sports Club. Dunn, a fellow Wisconsinite, was a good-hearted soul who let us park our Mokes at his place when we left town and put us up on his floor if we needed to spend the night. Dan's house was always open. He had amenities in his house like electricity, running water, and flush toilets, luxuries we did not have. Not having any way to call ahead, we let ourselves in and took over the place. One person got into the bathtub or enjoyed the toilet, one turned on the stereo, and a third raided the refrigerator. Dan complained all the time, but he was good-natured enough to understand our misery in the bush. I even invited tourists to stay at his place. He never turned them down, but he occasionally told me not to send any more visitors. Dunn was, after all, also living on a Peace Corps salary.

Volunteers developed what I called "the minimalist Peace Corps culture." We could comfortably sleep on any floor. We could eat an entire meal out of a tin cup. Of course, we did have dishes, but sometimes only washed them when we needed them. Many of us learned to use squat toilets and water instead of toilet paper. A cold shower out of a bucket or pan was quite sufficient. If we lacked a water filter where we lived, we developed a habit of throwing the bottom quarter of a glass of water away.

The Eldoret Theatre Club once asked me to be in a play. As a member of a jury in the play, I had no lines. When I showed up late one evening, someone from the audience had taken my place. No lines and easily replaced by a walk-on from the audience was the story of my acting life!

I waited in the reception area until the intermission. There was a tall, athletic Kenyan also waiting there for some reason. We struck up a conversation. He never introduced himself, just asked me questions about my Kenya experience.

I soon realized during our conversation that the man was Kipchoge Keino, the famous Kenyan runner. Among his many achievements was defeating the U.S. miler Jim Ryun in the 1500 meters at the 1968 Mexico City Olympics. We had a nice conversation about my work and international affairs. A few months later, I met him again outside of his sports shop on Oginga Odinga Street. Keino established a farm for orphaned boys west of Eldoret. I stopped at the farm in 2016, but Keino had left for the day.

I met another Kenyan Olympic gold medalist, Julius Korir, on his farm in Nandi during my 2016 project there. Korir won the steeplechase in Los Angeles in 1984. The Kalenjin tribe, including Keino and Korir, has produced many Olympians and many marathoners.

One day, George Roemer and I decided to have a good lunch in Eldoret at the Lincoln Hotel. There was an older white waiter in the dining room having a long conversation with an older white woman at one of the tables. The waiter apologized for not responding to us more quickly. "I was talking to Miss Markham over there. She is quite a famous woman!" he said. We did not know it at the time, but Miss Markham was Beryl Markham (1902-86, Wikipedia), a horse trainer for Lord Delamere and other notables, a famous Kenya bush pilot, and the first person to fly the Atlantic solo and from east to west (*West With The Night*, book by Beryl Markham).

CHAPTER 43—MY TOWN

On Fridays, I reported to my district agriculture officer, James Maina, in Kitale. I provided a written report covering my farm visits and other extension activities. I got to know Kitale very well. My weekly Kitale trip usually included a visit to the Standard Bank to make a withdrawal, a visit to the post office, purchases of camera film at D.V. Shah, and lunch at the Trans-Nzoia Bakery. At the beginning of the rainy season, trips to the Kenya Seed Company on the edge of Kitale to purchase seed for farmers were added to my to-do list.

I initially established my bank account at the Standard Bank in Eldoret, but few or none of the clients there would stand in a line. I did not like the pushing and shoving to get to the teller. Bob Kelly told me that it was better in Kitale. And it was. Kitale had rules. People formed queues.

Kitale rules had something to do with the remaining colonial residents still living there. Once, when I was in the post office and people started pushing, an older white woman turned around and gave everyone a dirty look. Order was restored immediately.

After I moved to Tongaren, there were so many requests for tree seedlings that the Forestry Department in Kitale became a frequent stop. A box of 50 seedlings cost only 2 Ksh. The usual tree requests included pine, eucalyptus, and cedar. I could fit four or five boxes in the Moke, depending on the number of passengers and other items. I made passengers hold tree boxes on their laps or secure them by hand on the flat sides on the Moke. I even remember putting a box of seedlings on the bonnet (hood) that I held while I drove with the other hand.

I am not sure of the reasons, but farmers in my district were quite enthusiastic about planting trees, especially in their home-steads and around the perimeters of their farms. Farmers told me that trees brought rain. Foresters told me that the many Eucalyptus trees planted by the colonial farmers had the negative effect of drawing too much moisture from ground water.

Nonetheless, on my later return trips, I was delighted to see so many trees and so many tall ones. Open vistas that I had viewed in the 1970s were no longer there. A famous Kenyan woman, Wangari Maathai, won the Nobel Peace Prize in 2004 for her efforts in pro-moting conservation and tree planting (Wikipedia).

In 1973, Kitale was building a new museum. Colonel Stoneham established a private museum in Kitale in 1924, the first of its kind in the country (Wikipedia). After Stoneham died in 1966, the Kenya government decided to build a new museum to incorporate his and other collections. Renamed the Kitale Museum or National Museum of Western Kenya, it opened in 1974.

It was not open before I left; however, I visited it a few times when I was in town in 1973. The young American woman who was organizing the place had been working with the Leakeys on their paleontological digs in the north around Lake Turkana and the Omo River. I do not recall why she changed jobs. She contacted the Peace Corps, and they took her on to work in the museum. It was the only time I ever saw the Peace Corps take on a volunteer already in country and not have the person go through the normal recruitment and training routine.

The many items I saw in the museum included an insect collection from Stoneham. I remember the butterflies, an impressive collection. I later joked to a friend concerning my extensive photo album collection that I planned to donate for a historical library back home. "If they can start a museum with a butterfly collection," I said, "then someone can start a library with my album collection!"

There was a young man who came up to me several times in Kitale during my first year in Kenya, begging for money. He said that his mother had died, and he needed money for the funeral. I did not believe him but gave him some coins anyway. The next time he had some other excuse. He subsequently forgot which story he used for which person he asked. Later, when he came up to me again saying that his mother had died, I asked him how many mothers he had. He turned away.

The man disappeared. About six months later, I was in Nairobi on Kenyatta Avenue when the same man came up to me begging for money. He did not recognize me at first. I asked him rather tersely if business was better in Nairobi than in Kitale. He hurried away.

PART IV—NAIROBI

CHAPTER 44—WHERE
CULTURES COLLIDE

I went to Nairobi, 240 or so miles away from my work site, about once every three months. I left my Moke at Dan Dunn's house in Eldoret and hitchhiked. My reasons for going varied, but included updating my vaccinations, other Peace Corps business, or just relaxing.

When in Nairobi, I typically stayed at another volunteer's house, usually with Mark Marquardt in Nairobi or Tammy Taylor in Ruiru. Sometimes I stayed with Dave Redgrave, the agriculture program director for the Peace Corps, in Westlands. I stayed in a cheap hotel only once or twice.

The Peace Corps office was next to Jevanjee Gardens, a two-block-square plaza west of downtown. During lunchtime, Jevanjee Gardens was inevitably dominated by soapbox speakers, usually trying to save souls.

Vic Preston Junior's Shell petrol station was around the corner from the Peace Corps office and next to Uhuru Highway. Preston was a rally race car driver from a rally racing family (Rally Wikia /

Vic Preston). He competed in the East African Safari Rally. I never heard that he ever won. He had a reputation of being courteous to other drivers, even sacrificing his own position in the race to help another driver out.

The University of Nairobi, the only university in the country at the time, was also located nearby. I walked around campus one day. When I used a men's room, I discovered that the fixtures said, "K of K, USA." Those fixtures were from the Kohler Company near Sheboygan, Wisconsin, just ten miles from where I grew up.

There was a police station right next to the university. Its location, in my opinion, was no accident. Student protests were always a huge headache for African heads of state, sometimes precipitating events that brought governments down.

I frequently walked to the New Stanley Hotel downtown to have breakfast at the Thorn Tree Restaurant. I first bought an *International Herald Tribune* at the news stand on the corner and then sat down to treat myself to an apple pie a la mode. Other than occasional mail from home, the Tribune was my only source of American sports news for months at a time. For entertainment, I read some of the notes left on the message board wrapped around the famous thorn (acacia) tree in the outdoor dining area.

While sitting at the Thorn Tree, I watched absurd tourists running around in their safari outfits, getting into zebra-striped VW buses to head out to the game parks. The waiters at the Thorn Tree never seemed to write anything down, just taking orders by memory no matter how complex they were. They seldom missed anything, but when they did, tourists could be obnoxious.

Whatever the problem, I sided with the waiters. I found American tourists were only exceeded by the Germans in their rudeness to the waiters. On a couple of occasions, I almost got up to tell the Americans where to go but thought better of it. I once apologized to the waiters on behalf of my fellow countrymen after the Americans left. Although I was hardly ever in town, some of the waiters recognized me when I did show up. They became my friends.

When in Nairobi, I often purchased my Ektachrome and Kodachrome film at the Asian shop under the Hilton nearby. Once I stood behind a tourist who was told by the Asian shopkeeper that he would give him a special price of 45 Ksh per roll. After the tourist happily paid and left, I offered 26 Ksh per roll for the same film, a price I knew well, and got it without any complaint from the shopkeeper.

Nairobi was safer in those days. I sometimes went to the late movie in the downtown area, and then walked two miles to a friend's house at midnight without incident. It was in Nairobi that I saw "Love Story" for the first time. One evening, there was a kung fu movie. When it let out, some Japanese tourists happened to be walking by. Movie goers coming out crossed over to the other side of the street to avoid the Japanese, who had no idea what was going on. I just laughed.

The mayor of Nairobi was Margaret Kenyatta, the eldest daughter of the president. She was tough and effective from everything I heard. On one of our days in Nairobi during training, we were taken on a tour of the city by a Peace Corps staff member. We drove through Mathari Valley, the famous slum. Most of the structures people lived in were made of plywood or pallets. Immigrants to the city, looking for a better life than on the *shamba* (farm), often ended up living in the slum because they could not find that dream job. Even if they did, the pay was often too low to support an apartment, much less a house.

In 1972, Mayor Kenyatta decided the slum had to go. She gave its residents a week to move out, had everything bulldozed into a pile, and then burned. Within a week, the slum started rebuilding again.

On a later work assignment in Kenya in 1996, a Ministry of Agriculture employee complained to me about the cost of living in Nairobi on his meager salary. "We do not get any raises," he complained. "When I started in the ministry with a new wife, we rented a three-bedroom flat. When we had a child, we had to move into a two-bedroom flat. By the time we had second child and my wife had a job, we could only afford one bedroom. No wonder some government workers take bribes!"

CHAPTER 45—OUT OF
AFRICA AND BACK AGAIN

In 1971, during my second year in country, while I was waiting for a bus on Ngong Road near Uhuru Highway, I kept noticing buses coming from a suburb called "Karen." I figured that Karen, like Nairobi, was probably a Maasai word from the olden days when the Maasai occupied the area. Nonetheless, I asked a Kenyan woman standing next to me if she knew where the name came from. "I am not real sure," she said, "but I heard that Karen was a white woman who once lived there and wrote a lot of nice things about Africa."

That inspired my interest in Karen. Who was this white woman who had a huge suburb of Nairobi named after her? The more I learned about Karen, the more she became a hero to me. Karen Dinesen, married for a short time to a Swede, Bror von Blixen, used the pen name Isak Dinesen when she wrote the book "Out of Africa" about her two decades in Kenya as a coffee farmer. I have seen the 1985 movie made from the book, starring Meryl Streep and Robert Redford, at least 20 times. I have read most of Karen's books, visited her museum home in Kenya and in her native Denmark, and the

Dinesen cabin in Mole Lake, Wisconsin on the Wolf River where her father hunted and trapped with Native Americans in the 1870s.

Alan Johnston, who was back living in Kenya when the movie was made, is seen twice in the movie as an extra. He played a white settler coming into Nairobi to join the war effort and then, later, celebrating the end of the war on the terrace of the Norfolk Hotel (notes from Johnston).

Beryl Markham, who George and I saw in Eldoret, was a figure in Karen's life in Kenya, and lived to see the movie made. Every time I traveled through Naivasha and saw the signs pointing to the Delamere Estates, a large property and farm still there today, I was reminded of a substantial colonial history that brought together a very interesting cast of characters.

The movie was part of the reason for my return to Kenya in 1987. As inspiring as the movie may have been to me, it was still a story about colonial Kenya, written from a white perspective. Kenya benefits from the tourism generated from the movie, but not necessarily from the memories of a less-desirable past.

Chapter 46—Country Cool

The urban Peace Corps experience is different in several ways when compared to the rural one. My Nairobi colleagues usually lived in apartments. They paid higher rent with a higher cost-of-living allowance than I received. Several of my rural colleagues, including myself, lived in abandoned British mansions for free. Peace Corps Kenya had two or three different levels of cost-of-living allowances. Later, when I served in Paraguay, there were seven.

I felt that the rural experience in Kenya was richer. My Swahili was better than that of my urban colleagues. I had more daily contact with Kenyans and less contact with volunteers or other foreigners. In fact, the longer I stayed in Kenya's rural areas, the more comfortable I was with Kenyans, and the less comfortable I was with my white colleagues, some of whom became cynical or complained too much.

I did miss out on urban opportunities. Some of my Nairobi colleagues were able to watch the replay of the NFL Football Game of the Week at a fancy bar on Kenyatta Avenue. One who worked in the Ministry of Agriculture in Nairobi got to write a draft speech for President Kenyatta. I never played golf at any of Kenya's golf courses, usually frequented by white residents or tourists, but also never had any desire to do so.

CHAPTER 47—THUMBING AROUND

G eorge and I found out early that the best way to get back and forth from Nairobi was to get out on the highway and hitchhike. We were not allowed to take our Mini Mokes out of our work or repair service area. I reported to my boss on most Fridays in Kitale 20 miles away. George and I were permitted to drive to our district headquarters, if necessary, 50 miles to Kakamega for him, 40 miles to Bungoma for me, and to our provincial office in Kakamega. I remember reporting to Bungoma only once.

We could not use our Mokes to go as far as Nairobi. We did that once to attend the Nairobi Agricultural Show in 1970, and almost had the Moke repossessed by the Peace Corps. Whenever we went to Nairobi, we drove to Eldoret and then hitchhiked the 200 miles to Nairobi from there.

The Peace Corps did not want us hitchhiking, of course, but they wanted us to occasionally show up in Nairobi for routine vaccinations, or briefings to our program leaders. Several staff knew we were hitchhiking; however, no one in the Peace Corps office ever said anything to me about it. This was the 1970s and hitchhiking was, in some corners, still cool.

The travel alternatives were discouraging, if not bleak. Local, what I called *wananchi* (citizen) buses, were slow and crowded. There were many stops. There seemed to be no limits on numbers of passengers. What about bathroom breaks? There was no guarantee that the bus would leave on time or that one going a long distance would arrive at a scheduled time. Either we were not aware of a comfortable express bus from Eldoret to Nairobi, if it existed, or did not care enough to locate it.

The local buses were the typical ones famous around the world for chickens, goats, crying babies, nursing mothers, and bundles of anything in the racks or hanging down the sides. Some people in the Peace Corps may have said that riding these buses added to the richness of the cultural experience. My opinion was that living in the countryside and doing extension work added up to plenty of culture. Most of the volunteers and staff living in Nairobi knew what we were experiencing but were certainly not living it.

The growing *matatu* system, another form of public transport, also crowded, could be quite dangerous. *Matatus* were pickup trucks with coverings over the back made either of metal or canvas. There was no required seating limit at the time, so these vehicles would stuff as many passengers into them as possible, often with people hanging outside on the back. There were many accidents.

The other option was the Rift Valley Peugeot (RVP) service, usually employing nine-passenger station wagons. I took the RVP twice, once from Mombasa after training and once from Nairobi to Eldoret. They typically drove around 90 miles an hour. Accidents were frequent. On my second and last trip with RVP, we came upon another RVP near Naivasha that had just crashed. There were bodies everywhere. It appeared that no one had survived. RVPs were often called RIPs or flying coffins.

Flagging for rides in rural Kenya was common as people had

few private cars or little money. No actual thumbing here, however. The ride sign was a slow waving of one arm toward the ground. It was easy for a white person to get a comfortable ride on the highways, but difficult for an African to get the same type of ride.

My hitchhikes were quite interesting and almost never risky. I got one with a big-game, safari hunting guide named John who lived most of the year in Southern Rhodesia. Among his past clients were Princess Margaret and Jimmy Stewart. One ride was a Kenya Safari Rally car, Number 68, not racing at the time, of course, and driven by a young British fellow. He was quite comfortable driving between 80-100 mph. I felt safe in his car. Everyone, including the foot police along the way, gave him a thumbs-up. It was my fastest single ride ever from Eldoret to Nairobi, taking about two-and-one-half hours.

Rally drivers were well-respected, even though some of them reputedly broke the rules during the official event. Jackson took a lot of interest in the rally. There were rumors that at least one crew switched out engines under trees out of sight in the bush to get more horsepower between the 24-hour inspections. According to Jackson, the engine switch took less than 45 minutes. The practice of hiring locals to fell trees across roads in front of the cars behind a cheating driver was apparently common.

The Asian Sikhs who gave me rides had nice cars and inevitably drove much faster than the speed limit. When I asked one of them why he drove so fast, his answer was, "It doesn't matter. When your time is up, it's up!" He did not accept any discussion of probability, stating that his religion did not accept the concept, at least not for driving.

I did, however, also get rides from Kenyans. They tended to drive more carefully as many had older cars. Kenyans were always curious to know where I was from, what I was doing, and how I liked the country.

George mentioned getting picked up by a cabinet minister. Another time he got a ride with a British military convoy on its way to the Uganda border to help Kenya guard against any potential incursion by Idi Amin.

I kept a record of my hitchhikes. In Kenya, I hitchhiked about 130 times for 5,500 miles, almost all of them between Eldoret and Nairobi. It was easier to get from Eldoret to Nairobi than from Nairobi to Eldoret. Nonetheless, I never failed to make the 200 miles between the two cities in one day. It usually took two or three rides with connections required in Naivasha, Nakuru or the turn-off to Kericho. Rides straight through were rare. On two occasions, it took me eight rides. I was never stranded in one place for more than an hour.

There was a road sign in the middle of Nakuru that had multiple arrows pointing to different cities of the world with the distances in kilometers listed. It had London, Cairo, Johannesburg, Nairobi, and other cities on it. I remember seeing it and took a photo that I now cannot seem to find. The Peace Corps used the sign with a volunteer standing next to it as a recruitment poster.

George and I never hitchhiked together, though, because we had different schedules, and it was more difficult for two people to get a ride. After George got married during our second year, he bought a private car.

The chances of getting picked up by someone I knew while hitchhiking was never going to be high, of course, but increased the longer I stayed. Kenya in the early 1970s had few main highways and not so many cars, yet I was picked up by someone I knew between Nairobi and Eldoret four times during my last year in country.

CHAPTER 48—SEE YOU AT YOUR SITE

D r. Bernard Easterday from the University of Wisconsin accompanied us to Kenya. Both Dr. Lee Swan and Dr. David Wieckert arrived in Kenya during the next two years to visit the Wisconsin volunteers. They were the organizers of the Peace Corps Kenya project on the UW-Madison Campus.

Unless necessary, I did not go into the Peace Corps office. I remember once going in two days in a row, then being questioned the second time why I was not back at my site. The country directors, three Black Americans while I was in Kenya, were very friendly and good people to work for, as well as our program director. However, there were some lower-level people in the office that I thought were best avoided.

Peace Corps cultures varied from country to country and from director to director. I served in two countries and visited another dozen or so Peace Corps offices around the world. There were country directors who would not remove so-called "problem" volunteers, trying instead to work things out. There were others who tried to weed out underperforming volunteers or send them home for various infractions. It seems that some directors were put on this earth to keep everyone in the fold, and others were meant to clean house.

When I was in Paraguay a few years later, my situation and the atmosphere there were different from the one in Kenya. I was an urban volunteer living in the suburbs of the capital, sometimes visiting the Peace Corps office every week. One of my unplanned but useful projects was to co-manage the photography lab at the office and teach other volunteers darkroom techniques. There was a library at the office with meeting tables. Volunteers were encouraged to interact, discuss problems, and bring issues to program leaders.

During my six years in the Peace Corps, I knew roughly 250 volunteers in the field. There were no real "problem" volunteers, but there were volunteers who had problems. All volunteers I knew tried to do their work. A few developed psychological or medical issues. A few had trouble adapting to their jobs or sites. A few had conflicts with co-workers or colleagues.

The Peace Corps in the 1960s provided a book collection referred to as a "book locker" to each volunteer. By 1970, the practice had ended; however, remnants of the lockers were found with older volunteers. J.R.R. Tolkien's book *The Hobbit* and the three books of his *Trilogy—Lord of The Rings* were real favorites. I read *The Hobbit* and left it at that. George got so hooked on the series that he took a couple of days off from work to read them. He was not the only volunteer who got hooked.

PART V—TONGAREN

CHAPTER 49—GOING NATIVE

After my home leave to the United States from October-November of 1972, George, Sue, and I decided to move out of Bettington. The Roemers moved to a house in Soy Village on the Eldoret to Kitale highway that was closer to Sue's teaching job in Eldoret.

My intention was to live closer to the center of my working area. I already had office space in Tongaren, which was the district headquarters for my area. There was no housing in Tongaren, however, so I decided to build my own African mud house. I asked for a small plot in the village on condition that I would donate my house to the village when I left. The district officer accepted my offer.

While I was building my Tongaren house, Jackson and I temporarily moved in with David Johnson just a couple miles north toward Ndalu in another former colonial house. David was a Peace Corps water engineer, as mentioned, also from Wisconsin.

Also living in the same house was Johnson's water project headman, a Luo. The headman slept around a lot. Luo men were not circumcised. Some Luhya women were curious to know what it would be like to have sex with an uncircumcised man, so he was not short of action. Once, when his wife came to stay with him, he brought home another woman, made his wife sleep on the floor, and then made his wife cook breakfast for each of them. When Jackson saw this, he berated the headman.

Jackson told me that another Luo man had once lived in the area. The Luhya men got tired of the Luo's sexual escapades. One night they got him so drunk that he passed out. When he woke up, he discovered that he was circumcised. He was irate. This probably ruined his standing and sexuality as a Luo man.

Some of my Peace Corps friends, upon hearing about my proposed house, asked me, "Are you going native?" Perhaps I was. I was into my third year in Kenya and was feeling more and more comfortable every day with my existence there.

I started my house by measuring out an 18x30-foot rectangular building. The house was large by Kenyan standards at the time. It was also unusual in being square rather than round, although square houses were certainly coming into style.

Building the house turned out to be a lot of work. Almost all my part of the work was done after hours since I had a day job to do. The 12 hours of daylight near the equator in Kenya gave me ample time to work on the house later in the day.

I hired a *fundi*, a young man, to locate, purchase, and cut down three smaller Eucalyptus trees for my poles and cross pieces, and then to thatch my roof. Jackson and I found a source of free swamp grass for thatch, common in the Tongaren area near the Nzoia River, and began cutting grass with *simis* (curved knives). I rigged a carrier on my Mini Moke to haul the grass. Grass is light and bulky, of course, so I had to make many trips from the swamp to my house. Then I had to haul my trees (poles and branches).

Life would have been easier had I been able to find two implements, a scythe for cutting the grass, and a post-hole digger to set my poles for the house. I described a scythe to Jackson.

"Hapana iko" (there is none), Jackson replied in his upcountry lingo. "There is no such thing in Kenya, at least not around here."

Likewise, there was no post-hole digger. Jackson suggested that I go to the Kenya Farmers Association (KFA) to find such devices. I did and was told that scythes and post-hole diggers had existed during colonial times. There was no longer any demand or supply. Such things were perhaps too expensive for the average Kenyan farmer, while back-breaking labor was apparently still cheap. I was hoping that some enterprising Kenyan entrepreneur would step up to re-invent them, but that did not happen. "Opportunity missed," I considered later. I surely could have myself found an entrepreneur somewhere to start a business making scythes and post-hole diggers.

I had to dig my pole holes for my house with a section of pipe, scooping the dirt out of the holes with my hands after loosening it with the pipe. Once I had the poles in, I secured them with a ridge plate made of 2x4s. I set my doors and window frames with 2x4s also. The 2x4s and boards for the doors and windows were made of pine, easy to work with and relatively cheap by my standards.

The next step was to attach the longer, slender Eucalyptus branches as main roof supports, fastened with wires. The roof was a four-sided, mansard design. The thinnest branches then were used across the roof to hold the thatch and across the inner and outer sides of the walls to hold the mud. The locals suggested about a 33-degree pitch to the roof.

One needs to put the roof on first, or at least an overhang before mudding the walls, because the rainy season will wash away unprotected mud walls. Once I had the roof on and the sticks to hold the mud in the walls, it was time to start the mud work. I worked on the house over several months in late 1972 and early 1973 during the dry season.

I had plenty of soil in my backyard for mud. But making the mud was difficult. I had to dig a pit and keep pouring water into it. The mud was kneaded with bare feet. It became apparent that I could not do this alone, even with Jackson helping me. Both Jackson and the district officer on site, a Kalengin named Kip Lang'at, suggested I get help.

Lang'at told me that he could round up some tax dodgers to help me. People were required to pay an annual head or pole tax. They had to carry a receipt on them if they paid. Those who did not pay were seldom charged or fined but would be subject to occasional work duties for the municipalities. Lang'at offered to find those people for my house project.

"Finding tax dodgers will be easy," said Lang'at. "They hang out in the bars, even in the morning." So, he and I jumped into his Land Rover and headed to the nearest bar. We made two such trips, finding about a dozen laborers. One of my laborers was a rather well-to-do farmer who I had visited in the area. He told me that he did not like paying taxes. He looked rather embarrassed to be caught up in my house-building project, and especially to be doing the lowly task of mudding. I humored him to make him feel better.

My role for mudding was to drive back and forth from the river to fetch water, using a barrel in the back seat of my Mini Moke. More than once at the river, I encountered women washing clothes. Some of them, not thinking I was coming back, were washing their own garments while topless. When they saw me coming, they hurried to cover up. We were all embarrassed at first, but then they just laughed.

With the free labor, I got most of the interior mud in the walls done in two days. Jackson and I continued to do some mudding when we had time. I never finished the final mudding, however, nor did I ever plaster the walls. Nonetheless, the walls were sufficient for my purposes. The house cost me about $200 to build.

The house had two bedrooms, one for me and one for Jackson. There was a kitchen in the back and a living room in the front. I built my own furniture out of pine. These included two beds, a table and two chairs.

By May of 1973, when the rainy season began, I had been living in the house for a couple months. Unfortunately, the grass roof leaked in several places. The advice I had gotten from the locals, that the pitch of the roof at 33 degrees was sufficient to allow rain to run off, turned out to be incorrect. Even Jackson did not have any better advice.

Jackson and I concluded that the roof had to be raised to at least 45 degrees. Fortunately, there were sticks and grass left over to extend the roof. We called the *fundi* back to remove the grass down to just over the mud walls so I could re-do the roof supports. I undid the sticks on the upper part of the roof and down the four corners of the roof. I took a long horizontal pole and two supports to push up the roof from the inside of the house to the appropriate angle. I extended all the sticks to the peak and quickly rewired everything. The *fundi* then rethatched the roof. The roof did not leak after that.

The repair took only a few days, but I missed a potential trip with several Peace Corps friends to Turkana District in the north to view a total eclipse of the sun. There was only a partial eclipse in Tongaren. The sky was cloudy and just darkened somewhat.

The Kenya government announced the eclipse on the radio for several days in advance, telling people not to panic. Most Kenyans knew what an eclipse was or at least did not regard it as anything to be concerned about. Nonetheless, the less-literate tribes, mostly in the north, could regard such an event as a bad omen. There was a rumor that a tribal *shaman* had committed suicide.

The mud house had wooden shutters on the windows but no

panes or screens. If I wanted to air out the house, I had to open the shutters. I closed them during the day when I was gone. At night they were open until I went to sleep. My only light was a Petromax pressure lamp that ran on kerosene. Mosquitoes did not like the smell. Beetles, about an inch long or more with large pincers, however, were attracted by the light. They flew in, bounced off the glass and fell unto the table or the book I happened to be reading near the light. I threw the beetles back out the window. They inevitably came back.

I decided to test the pincer strength of the large beetles. Grabbing a beetle from behind, I let it grab the edge of the book by its pincers, and then lifted the beetle and the book. Those beetles could easily lift a half-pound book. I repeated this experiment with other items on the table. One would not have wanted a beetle to grab one's finger!

One night, I was standing outside of the house with Jackson when a chorus of dog howls passed from the distant east through the village and off toward the west. "*Mbwa wana sema nini?*" (what are the dogs saying), I asked Jackson.

Inaweza kua chui. " (it could be a leopard), Jackson replied. "It could be as far away as the Cherangani Hills, about 30 miles to the east. The dogs are just spreading the message in all directions."

I used the communal squat toilet located near my house in Tongaren. It was small, square mud building above a bore hole, called a "long-drop," about ten feet deep, with a wooden platform and slot in the top. I used my own toilet paper. It would take several years to fill the hole. Once full, the toilet would be relocated to another spot.

CHAPTER 50—SNAKES ON THE PLAIN

Kenya was home to plenty of nasty snakes, including puff adders, spitting cobras, and mambas. On our second day in the country, several of us went to visit the National Museum in Westlands, a suburb of Nairobi. The snake park was also there. In addition to tourist revenue, snakes were used to collect venom to produce anti-venom. Except for having seen an African snake or two in a zoo in the United States, this was the first time I remembered seeing most of these snakes.

I swear the black mamba at the park was at least ten feet long! Black mambas typically live in the savannah, although their habitat varies. It is a gray snake with a black mouth. The black mamba is often considered the deadliest snake in Africa, but they do not kill as many people as puff adders, which are more numerous and live closer to people. However, black mamba venom is very lethal, and these snakes can be aggressive. Instead of trying to escape, black mambas will sometimes chase and attack, often moving as fast as a human can run. Green mambas, their deadly cousins, live in trees and are a menace to fruit pickers.

Kenyans joked that the black mamba was a two-step snake and

the green mamba a three-step snake because that is how long you live after being bitten. That is not true. Realistically, if bitten by a black mamba, a human may have a half hour to live.

On farm visits when we were touring the fields, I played it safe. The farmer led the way, of course. I let the agriculture assistant follow him. In third place, I figured if the farmer stirred up a snake, it would bite the farmer or my assistant before it would bite me!

Each Peace Corps volunteer was issued a medical kit, a gray metallic box that also contained a snake-bite kit. We were instructed to keep the medical kit handy, usually in the house. George and I kept the snake-bite kits in our Mokes. The kits did not contain anti-venom, just tourniquets, a lancet, and instructions about how to suck out venom. Fortunately, we never had to use the kits.

The program director for the agriculture volunteers, David Redgrave, came to visit his volunteers several times. Once he and George were driving in the schemes when they encountered a large snake crossing the road. Dave stepped on the brakes of his Land Rover just as he was crossing the snake, cutting it in three pieces. George did not remember what kind it was.

I saw about a dozen snakes in my four years in Kenya, most of them while driving on backroads. I saw them almost always in October or November, the beginning of the dry season, when snakes were moving toward rivers and other sources of water. I once saw a three-foot green snake cross the road in front of my Moke into a homestead, so I stopped to tell the people that there was a snake on the premises.

One report of an unusual case of a dead cow came from Soysambu Scheme near Bettington when I first arrived. The veterinary assistant could not figure out why a healthy cow just suddenly died. Then he saw two small puncture wounds in the cow's nose. A poisonous and likely large snake had killed the cow. A panic spread in the community when the cause of the cow's death was determined. I heard nothing further about the incident.

I heard another story a year later that a girl in Kamukuywa Scheme, about 20 miles away, died after she was bitten by a snake while relieving herself on some rocks near her house. Several members of the family took *jembes* (hoes) and *pangas* (machetes), dug the snake out and hacked it to pieces. The man telling the story said he thought it was a mamba. Western Kenyans did not tolerate snakes of any kind. They killed every snake they saw, venomous or not.

One day at my house in Tongaren, I heard a bird squawking very loudly in a tree near my house. "This bird is telling us there is snake nearby," Jackson said. The next morning, there was a small green snake curled up in a crack in a wall in my house. Taking no chances, I killed the snake and tossed it outside. It was the only snake I ever killed in Kenya. As much as I feared snakes, I hated killing them. I was no expert on identifying them. Any snake that was not green was probably poisonous, but some of the green ones were, too.

CHAPTER 51—CHEWING UP THE PLACE

I did not bother to do what all Kenyans did to keep termites out of their houses. Kenyans scraped away the grass to establish a hard barrier around the house, usually about ten feet out, and plastered it with a mixture of manure, sand, and cement. The reason for this was to keep a hard, bare area to prevent insects and other vermin from sneaking up to the house. Especially, during the day, chickens and other birds picked off any offending vermin.

This barrier was particularly effective against termites, who would eat the soft timbers and grass roof. Not liking light and fearing predators, termites needed to move in tunnels or just below the surface. They could not easily approach the house through the hard surface. They would not make it to the house if they traveled over the top.

Because I did not create the barrier, I had termites in my house. My support posts and crosspieces, still exposed for lack of the final mudding, were made of Eucalyptus, not attractive to termites. But the termites, after entering the house, would crawl up the posts to get at the pine wood windows and other framework and then to the grass roof. Wherever they went, termites constructed thin mud tunnels to cover themselves.

I discovered that painting the posts with old engine oil was generally effective in keeping the termites off. When the oil dried in a few weeks, however, termites began their upward journey again.

I accidentally discovered an unusual trap for the termites. Because I was always making something out of pine wood, like my furniture, I kept boards and two-by-fours stacked against the inside wall near the entrance.

One day I came home and heard a kind of *wah-wah* sound from the boards. The termites had made tunnels in the small spaces between the boards and were chewing away shallow grooves in the pine. The sound they made, a kind of distress warning when I came into the room, was apparently their signal to move to safety. Too late for them, I turned the boards over and painted them with engine oil, killing thousands of termites at a time. I continued to do this every few weeks, leaving some boards as bait, for the whole year I lived in the house. The termites never got to my windows, framework, or roof.

Jackson, like the many other maize farmers in western Kenya, built a maize storage shed on his farm. The shed usually had a screen-mesh siding to keep birds and other larger creatures out. It was built on two or three-foot stilts to raise it above the ground. Upturned metal bowls were placed on top of each stilt before the building was constructed above it, or metal flanges were wrapped around the stilts. The metal barriers kept mice, termites, and other vermin from crawling up and reaching the maize from below.

Jackson always complained about mice and termites. Mice not only ate the maize but chewed holes in most or all the burlap bags in the shed, even though they only needed one bag for nesting or to just access the maize in the bag. Termites took no interest in the maize, but just ate the burlap bags—again, not just one bag, but they inevitably preferred to attack every bag in the shed. "*Bure kabisa!*" (totally worthless), Jackson would always say.

CHAPTER 52—BECOMING
ONE WITH THE PEOPLE

L ife in my house in Tongaren was peaceful in 1973. The village was small, maybe 100 residents. There was a small circle of *maduka* (shops) that created a *soko* (market). There was a Catholic *kanisa* (church), a mud structure that I never entered. An Irish priest named O'Connor came for services on Sunday mornings. He sometimes came over to my house to say "Hello." I was the only white resident in the village. Tongaren allowed me to further distance myself from my white friends, something I wanted to do, and to get closer to my Kenyan friends.

Over time, the people of Tongaren accepted my presence. I regularly drank a morning *chai* or *kahawa* and ate a *mandazi* or two at the only place resembling a café or restaurant in the village before going to my office or visiting farms. People just called me "Otto." The children eventually no longer came up to me to stare, smile, or joke with the *mzungu*.

I thought nothing of my waning lack of celebrity until one morning when I was shaving. I looked in the mirror and suddenly realized that I was white! The people of Tongaren had let me forget I was white and that I was still a foreigner in their midst. It was a wonderful moment! I thought about it for several days.

When I first came to my site in western Kenya, I was clearly an *mzungu*, a white man no different than *wazungu* before me. Then I quickly became an American, unlike the British or colonial settlers from other countries that came before. Then I was not just any American, not a tourist, for example, but I became a *"mwana Peace Corps(e)"*, a member of a volunteer group called the Peace Corps. Finally, I became just "Otto." It was my third year in Kenya.

I often wondered if I could have made this transition to "Otto" had I stayed the normal two-year Peace Corps term. Perhaps I could have, but it was during my third year that I sensed a transition. I was now confident in my use of upcountry Swahili and was picking up some Kiluhya. I had finally figured out how to get things done on my job. I had made Kenyan friends. Certainly, much of the transition had really occurred in my head. No doubt, however, Jackson smoothed my way with the people and the culture in everything I did.

Tongaren had a meat market. This meant a hanging beef carcass in a fly-screened enclosure behind a counter. The vendor had three days to sell the meat. If I went the first day, the meat was fresh. If I went the third day, it was cheaper but not fresh. Whichever cut you got was wrapped in newspaper.

A cow or bull would be slaughtered once a week under a tree near the meat market with a sturdy branch to lift and then skin and gut the animal. The person who did the slaughtering was a Muslim who went from village to village. The reason was that the Muslims who lived in the area, although fewer in number, insisted that the animal be slaughtered properly and blessed. The Christians and traditionalists did not care.

During the long rainy season from April to August, it usually rained in the afternoon at about 2:00 p.m. On some days, there was no rain, or it would come at night. But usually it came in the afternoon and about five days per week. Getting caught in the rain doing farm visits or just driving around was no fun. I often had to wait it out under cover. One could get very wet in a Moke with no sides. The dirt roads became very slippery. Because the Moke was low to the ground, it could easily get hung up in truck ruts. Or it might just slide off the road into the ditch.

I slid off the road a half-dozen times. Twice, I was alone and unable to get back on the road. Suddenly, out of nowhere, several small boys would show up to help me, rubbing their fingers together and saying, "*Shilingi, shilingi!*" Five Ksh usually got me back on the road.

I soon figured out how to tell if it was going to rain. Mount Elgon was only about thirty miles away as the crow flies. If it clouded over by 10:00 a.m., it would rain that afternoon. If not clouded over, it would not rain, at least not in the afternoon. One could see the mountain from anywhere in the schemes. It was one of the few local things I figured out on my own.

One day I was standing outside and heard a flock of geese flying over. Sure enough, I looked up to see that they were flying in a V formation. I temporarily forgot where I was. For three years, I had not seen geese nor even thought about them. I was shocked to realize that I was indeed in Kenya and not in Wisconsin. They were Egyptian geese.

One of the first Peace Corps volunteers that Jackson worked for was Charles "Ben" Pike, who served from 1966-68. Jackson really liked him and always spoke highly of him. I had never met him. Then, in 1973, Jackson received a letter from Pike asking him to help with Pike's University of Wisconsin PhD study. Jackson explained to me what he could of the offer. Pike soon arrived in Tongaren to ask me if he could borrow Jackson for a month. He was doing his research on African folklore and wanted Jackson to interview elders in his home village in Kabras. I agreed that it was a good thing for Jackson to do. Pike paid him from his funding for the month, and I also paid Jackson as usual. I did not mind if Jackson took time off, which he also had to at times for his farm and family. He was often away. I was settled in at Tongaren.

Jackson's wife Angela had trouble getting pregnant at first. Finally, when she did and was about to give birth, she had problems. Jackson had to get a taxi to take her to the hospital in Eldoret. He then came to Tongaren on his bicycle in a panic to borrow some money from me. She was at the government hospital, he said, but they would not give her proper attention unless he bribed the doctor. In the end, Angela had her baby successfully.

Such was the state of government medicine in Kenya. Jackson always said that if the medical problem were small, a Kenyan doctor could probably fix it. If it were big, better go to a private, expensive Asian doctor. In any case, the bigger the problem, the more it would cost, even though the Kenya health care system was nominally free.

CHAPTER 53—SCHOLARLY EFFORTS

Government officials were sometimes asked to help local schools. I contributed some of my shillings to local school fundraisers, *harambee* efforts. I taught occasional classes at the Lugari Farmers Training Centre, including forages, cattle nutrition, and even a class in auto mechanics, using my Moke as a prop. The Centre was funded in part by the Quakers.

The British educational system required an exam to pass from Standard-7 to Form-1. The standard level was roughly equivalent to our grade school and the form level to our high school. Government employees could be asked to monitor such exams. I was called upon to monitor an exam in the Kimilili area in the Mount Elgon foothills. One of my assistants rode with me to visit the village in advance of the exam day.

When we arrived in the village, the younger children, who usually come running to check out the *mzungu*, stayed off in the distance just staring. *"Namna gani?"* (what is the matter), I asked my assistant.

"They have never seen a white man before," he said. I checked out the school, talked to the school administrator, and got the

Ministry of Education instructions for the exam day.

We repeated our trip on the day of the exam. I arrived early, exams, pencils, and timing watch in hand. The students sat at attention, almost pleasantly stunned. Their educational future hung in the balance. I read the ground rules for the exam and asked if there were any questions. There were none. I wished them well. The exam went smoothly.

I heard a few days later that almost all the students had passed. The school had set a record for success. There was a "thank you" letter for my service. I was told that the students did better on the exam that year because there was an *mzungu* in charge!

Most of the local primary schools were made of local materials like the houses—mud structures with grass roofs. There were long benches where students sat side by side. Desks, or rather writing surfaces, were also long benches, just elevated in front of students. Students wore uniforms, either blue, brown, or green in color, depending on the school and grade level.

Standard education required school fees, a burden for many rural families. Secondary education was paid by government. Putting children through primary school to get to secondary school was such a high priority that families in western Kenya were heard to sacrifice basic needs for school fees or even commit minor crimes to get the money. The Kenya government finally offered—around 1973, if memory serves me right—to make Standard 1-4 education free of charge.

CHAPTER 54—TO LIGHT A FIRE

Jackson and I often talked about the motivation of the Luhya people in contrast to other ethnic groups in Kenya. At the time, we still used the word "*kabila,*" which is usually translated as "tribe." Anthropologists were trying to get away from the general usage of "tribe" because of negative connotations.

Jackson could be hard on his own people. "We do not work as hard as the Kikuyus," Jackson said. "We do not push to earn money like the Kikuyus. We do not care for our cattle like the Kalenjin. We are not as proud of ourselves as the Luos are.

"There is a saying," Jackson continued. "Where there is a tree, a Luhya will find shade and sit down to rest. A Kikuyu will find an axe, cut the tree down, and sell the firewood.

"There is also an unfortunate hierarchy among the tribes," Jackson went on. "The Kikuyus think they are on the top and tribes like the Maasai and Turkanas are put at the bottom. Kikuyus will not work for (under) Luhyas, and Luhyas will not work for Turkanas, but Luhyas will work for Kikuyus, and Turkanas will work for Luhyas or Kikuyus. Kikuyus and Luos will work for Asians, but Luos will never work for Kikuyus."

Over time, I expressed some of my reservations about the lack of progress I saw in Luhya country to one of my favorite agricultural assistants, Peter Wamalwa. Wamalwa worked with me in Kiminini Settlement Scheme and I would often confide in him. When Wamalwa and I traveled together in the Kiminini, like other assistants, he typically took me to visit the more progressive farmers. He was, nonetheless, often very frustrated with many of his own people. "How do we light a fire under these people?" Wamalwa often asked.

One farm we visited was owned by a teacher who was away at the school when we arrived. His wife was at home digging with a *jembe* (hoe) in the garden. Two older sons were sitting on chairs under a tree. "Why aren't you helping your mother?" Wamalwa asked. The two sons had just finished secondary school, one at the Form-6 level and one at Form-4. "We are educated now," they said. "We don't have to do *kazi ya shamba* (farm work) anymore!"

Wamalwa complained to me later. "Anybody with any education these days aspires to get a desk job in Nairobi! If they go there, they will end up in the slums. They get lazy. Physical work is now beneath their dignity. They do not see the opportunities they have on the farm. They do not want to stay and contribute to the local community. Western Kenya is not glamorous enough!"

One midnight, Wamalwa bicycled all the way from his farm in Kabuyefwe to Tongaren, banging on my door to wake me up. Jackson was not there that night. "Get up!" he shouted. "We are finally going to see Luhyas working hard!"

"In the middle of the night?" I asked.

"Yes," he replied. "I will explain on the way."

We put Wamalwa's bicycle in the back of my Moke and headed to a farm in Naitiri Scheme. When we arrived, we found several farmers eagerly loading bags of maize onto a lorry headed for Uganda. Since Idi Amin had overthrown the government in Uganda, the country's economy had collapsed. Uganda was short of several commodities, including maize.

"You see how hard these farmers are working?" Wamalwa emphasized. "There are several things happening here. One is that Uganda next door is short of maize. The second is that farmers are being paid twice what they would receive from the cooperative, their only legal market under the Maize Marketing Board rules. The cooperative pays 40 Ksh per bag. The black-market price tonight is 80 Ksh per bag. The third thing is that they are being paid cash on the spot. The cooperatives are always late in paying the farmers."

"Incentives make all the difference!" Wamalwa continued. "There are too many controls on farmers! There is too much corruption within the cooperatives. There should be freer markets, more free-marketing."

I always knew that many local farmer cooperatives were either corrupt or incompetent. But when I saw this, I was more convinced by what Wamalwa said and what really made Kenyan farmers tick, so to speak.

Wamalwa had to assure the people in Naitiri that I was not a spy for the Kenya government. "You are not going report this," he demanded.

"Absolutely not!" I replied. "I imagine this is happening all over western Kenya as we speak."

When Jackson returned the next day, I told him what had transpired. Without saying much, Jackson was delighted. "*Kuna matumaini kwa sisi,*" (there is hope for us), he laughed.

When I returned to Kenya for the 2016 dairy cooperative project in Nandi, I was told that the World Bank and the IMF had persuaded Kenya in the 1990s to move away from cooperatives to private dairy haulers and processing companies. However, these private companies would sometimes go bankrupt, owing considerable money with little or no legal recourse for farmers. Nandi farmers were going back to forming dairy cooperatives with government backing.

CHAPTER 55—ANOTHER
RIVAL GOES DOWN

While I was in Kenya, another political tragedy occurred with the death of Ronald Ngala. Ngala was a Member of Parliament and Cabinet Minister from the Coast Province. In 1960, before full Independence in 1963, he and others formed the Kenya African Democratic Union (KADU), a political party that rivaled the existing Kenya African National Union (KANU) and other parties (Wikipedia).

KADU was dissolved in 1964 after losing several seats to KANU in elections. The remaining leaders of KADU, Masinde Muliro from the Luhya area, Daniel arap Moi from the Kalenjin area, and Ngala decided to join President Kenyatta's KANU. Moi later became vice president, and then the second president of Kenya. Ngala, however, despite his prominent positions in the Kenyatta-led government, was often an outspoken critic of the president.

In 1972, Ngala was traveling from Mombasa to Nairobi in advance of upcoming independence festivities on December 12. His driver lost control of the car, overturning several times. Ngala sustained head injuries and died on Christmas Day in the hospital. The driver at first stated that bees had entered the car and caused him to lose control. He later changed his story under oath during an investigation.

I heard the news of the accident on the radio. Ngala had been taken to a hospital and was initially not considered to be seriously hurt. When I heard the news, I told Jackson about it. Jackson's first comment was, "Which hospital is he in?" I answered that I was not sure but thought that Ngala had been taken to Kenyatta Hospital, considered a reasonably good medical facility at the time.

"Yeye ni kwisha!" (he is finished), Jackson retorted. "If he is in Kenyatta Hospital, the government will kill him there!"

"But they said that he was not badly hurt," I replied.

"Atakufa kweli!" (he will surely die), Jackson said again forcefully.

Reports on the radio over the next several days indicated that Ngala was out of imminent danger and likely to recover. Then, on Christmas Day, it was announced that Ngala had suddenly died. There was a rumor of diabetic complications.

"I told you so!" Jackson said. "Kenyatta is getting rid of his opponents." Jackson was in a sour mood for several days after that. He was certainly not alone in western Kenya in his distrust of the Kenyatta government. Again, the euphoria and optimism from independence were giving way to the realities of African politics.

Jackson always felt that the coastal Swahilis (Mijikendas) were more trustworthy and evenhanded politically because they were not part of upcountry tribal rivalries. I was not sure if that was true, but I know that Jackson liked Ngala for his opposition to Kenyatta. In his opinion, Ngala was a less volatile counterbalance to Kikuyu power than the Luos were.

In 1975, the year after I left Kenya, another Kenyatta opponent, J.M. Kariuki, a Kikuyu politician from the Nyeri area north of

Nairobi, was assassinated (Wikipedia). His body was found stabbed and lying on an ant hill along a rural road south of Nairobi. Kariuki, a Member of Parliament from Nyandarua, had once been a personal assistant to President Kenyatta. But later, he disagreed with Kenyatta on many issues. There were political disputes even within Kikuyu between the Gatundu or Nairobi area faction represented by Kenyatta, and the Nyeri faction, represented by Kariuki.

I had heard a lot about Kariuki. One Kenyan described him as a prototype of Robert Kennedy, someone who was handsome, youthful, popular, intelligent, eloquent, outspoken, and another potential future president.

"Pity poor Kenya!" I often thought over the years. "How many leaders must they kill in the name of power and stability?" Although Kenyans had every reason to be disgusted with their leadership and the extensive corruption that went with it, Kenya has managed to avoid the more-serious pitfalls of most of its neighbors.

Somalia, for example, was often considered to be the most failed state in the world (*The Economist*, October 2016). Civil wars, droughts, foreign interventions, and terrorism resulted in hundreds of thousands of deaths and additional hundreds of thousands living in refugee camps in Ethiopia and Kenya. I had the opportunity to visit two Somali refugee camps in Ethiopia in the 1990s. One had 60,000 residents at the time, but once had 360,000 residents at its peak population.

Somalia did not have a federal government of any significance for more than two decades. I told my conservative friends in America, who always seemed to be wanting to create a society with strong religious and family values, no federal government, no regulations, no taxes, and where everyone had guns, that they should, therefore, be careful what they wished for, because Somalia was just such an ideal place!

Ethiopia, another neighbor, suffered a military coup in 1974, a subsequent communist government, a civil war, several purges, and a couple of severe droughts (Wikipedia). Well over a million people died during the 17-year reign of Colonel Mengistu Haile Mariam. The northern Eritrea Province, with help from Tigray Province, broke off in 1991 and became independent in 1993. Approximately 5-6 million people from the north defeated the rest of Ethiopia, a country of 50 million people. I visited Ethiopia in 1972, again in 1974, and spent two years there from 1990-92. Eritrea has become another repressive dictatorship.

Sudan suffered through military coups and a civil war that lasted more than 30 years. South Sudan eventually split off to become independent. Several million people in South Sudan died. The new country is still in turmoil. The remaining nation of Sudan in the north then found itself engaged in a reputed genocide in Darfur.

Uganda suffered through a military coup under Idi Amin, a civil war and more military rule. Both Rwanda and Burundi had genocides. Only Tanzania, united under a Swahili and socialist banner and run by Julius Nyerere, one of the less-corrupted presidents in Africa, managed to keep things together.

Kenya has had a couple of attempted military coups that failed, one under Kenyatta just before I arrived, and the most noted one under Moi in 1982. Kenya, an economic powerhouse in East Africa with a substantial middle class, has always had too much to lose from a major political suicide. Kenya has managed to survive some very nasty presidential elections. Perhaps Kenya just lucked out. "We have gone to the abyss more than once," Kenyans would say. "We looked over the edge and always decided not to jump."

CHAPTER 56—OUTSIDE LOOKING IN

The local Member of Parliament (MP) for Tongaren was Elijah Mwangale who lived in Kimilili. I twice accompanied District Officer Kip Lang'at to visit Mwangale at his home. Mwangale was familiarly known as *Bwana Kiko* (Mister Pipe) because he frequently smoked a pipe (Wikipedia). He earned a Masters' degree at West Virginia University where he met his wife, a white American. Mwangale later became Minister of Agriculture, and then Minister of Foreign Affairs. He was at first a friend of fellow Luhya Minister Masinde Muliro, but later they were political enemies. With few exceptions, cabinet ministers were also members of parliament (MPs) from their home districts. While Mwangale became caught up in a scandal or two, Muliro was considered a straight shooter and, at the time of his sudden death of an apparent heart attack, a serious candidate for president (Wikipedia).

Muliro came to Tongaren one day to do a fundraiser for the local school. He used a technique common at the time to ask for money, according to Jackson. Muliro asked for a shilling from everyone who wore glasses, passed the hat, then asked for a shilling from those who were missing two or more teeth, then from those who wore a certain color that day, etc. It was quite effective. He even took me for a few shillings. I got to shake his hand.

As a foreigner, I was somewhat shielded from the repercussions of local and national politics in Kenya. After all, I could leave at any time and escape to another place called America. Jackson, like most Kenyans, could not. Fortunately, Kenya gave me close to four years of safety and tranquility.

I did not drink alcohol, smoke pot, or conduct myself in an otherwise disrespectful way. There were things one needed to know about that one might not care about in America. If one heard the Kenya national anthem, for instance, always played in theaters before a movie, one had better stand up, or get fined or thrown out of the theater. When a British resident named his dog Kenyatta, he was severely reprimanded and fined. So was a tourist leaving at the airport who decided to throw his extra Kenya currency into a trash can.

All public offices, government displays, and private businesses in Kenya were required to prominently display a framed photograph of the president of Kenya. A religious figure such as Jesus, the Virgin Mary, a Hindu deity, or the Aga Khan, for instance, may be displayed at the same level on the wall, but I never saw any image on a wall higher than that of the president.

There was censorship. The list of banned publications in Kenya included mostly revolutionary and communist literature like Mao Tse Tung's *Little Red Book*. *Playboy Magazine* was banned sometime in 1972. Other publications were constantly monitored. If an article criticized the president, his administration, or Kenya in general in *Time* or *Newsweek*, for instance, that week's issue was seized at the Nairobi airport or the Mombasa port. George and I subscribed to both magazines. A few issues went missing. We knew why because relatives in the United States who received the magazines asked us about the articles. Kenya also banned hippies in 1972 (*New York*

Times, March 12, 1972), not allowing tourists who looked like hippies to enter, and enforcing certain codes of dress and conduct within the country.

One MP proposed to ban the skin creams called "Ambi" and "Ambi Extra." Some of these products were skin lighteners. Kenyan women often used them, as did some men. The reason given for the proposed ban was that Africans should be proud of their color and not use skin lighteners. "The proposal failed because too many MPs used it themselves!" Jackson laughed. "Skin lighteners are very popular with Kenyan prostitutes," he added.

"Why is it that black people want to be lighter and white people sit in the sun to get darker?" I asked Jackson. "What is wrong with liking your own color? We should embrace who we are."

"*Labda nusu nyeusi na nusu nyeupe ni bora*" (perhaps half-black and half-white is better), Jackson replied.

Jackson and I frequently talked about Kenya politics. He complained endlessly about corruption, especially how all politicians seemed to become incredibly wealthy. "*Wanasiasa kula pesa nyingi!*" (politicians eat a lot of money), he said. "But there are two problems," he continued. "One is that we citizens allow our politicians to get away with corruption. The second is that, if I were a politician myself, I would likely do the same thing!"

CHAPTER 57—THE HARDEST PART

Leaving after two years was never easy for most volunteers. Leaving after three or four years was even more difficult. Kenya had become my home. With my mud house, increasing isolation from other volunteers, and comfort with the language and culture, several of my friends thought I was "going native" for sure. Had I met the right woman to share my life with, I might have indeed stayed. Twelve of the 48 original volunteers in my group extended for a third year. Two of them were still there after I left. At least two of them married Africans.

I saw several volunteers off. Sometimes we had a party. Sometimes we even went to the airport in Nairobi, but we seldom said goodbye. There were no hugs. It was mostly a kind of serene sadness. We realized that it was unlikely that most of us would ever see each other again, so why get emotional?

The old Embakasi Airport in Nairobi was quite the experience. There was little security. We could escort our friends directly to the gate. There were only a couple of gates on the first floor of a rather small terminal. On the second floor was a restaurant and open-air veranda where we could watch planes land and take off. The 747s went airborne right in front of the building, shaking the whole place considerably. We could smell the exhaust of the jet engines.

Jackson once went along with me to see someone off. He was awed. "*Ndege ni kubwa sana!*" (that is a very large plane), he said several times. Nowadays, at all major airports, things have surely changed. No more friends and relatives at the gate. No more up-close views of planes coming and going.

I left Tongaren in December of 1973 and moved back for my last two months with David Johnson, the 1972-74 water project volunteer. I sold or donated my Tongaren household possessions to Jackson.

Visiting my schemes and farmer friends for the last *kwaheris* (goodbyes) was hard. People gave me more than the usual quantity of bananas or pineapples. Many of them insisted on cooking a meal for me, usually a chicken, a dietary honor for someone of my status. I did not have to cook or even look for food for the last month.

At one farm, already running out of time and not hungry, I specifically asked my agricultural assistant to plead with the owner not to do anything special for me. "The usual two cups of chai would be fine," I demanded. I was getting tired of eating chicken. My assistant told me that I would have a hard time getting out of this one. Sure enough, when I arrived, children were chasing a poor hapless bird around the yard. In 45 minutes, I was eating the thing, a bit tough, but tasty as usual, with the common sides of *ugali* and *sukuma wiki*.

One of my last official acts was to turn in another annual report, my second, to my chain of command. The previous report contained the results of an extensive survey I had done in my eight schemes. The second one elaborated on certain areas with complaints and suggestions, especially targeted at the cooperatives and milk collection system. I kept copies of these reports.

Leaving Jackson was the most difficult. Tina and Angela were in tears. I turned out to be the last volunteer Jackson ever worked for. Of course, I expected to return to Kenya for a visit. That did not happen for another 13 years, but I kept in touch. Jackson expressed a desire to visit the United States, but never had any money. At the time, none of his Peace Corps friends had much money either. The idea kept getting put off. Jackson would never see the United States.

Once I got to Nairobi, I had to process my termination from the Peace Corps, turn in my Moke, get a medical clearance, get part of my readjustment allowance, and buy a ticket home.

I planned and then rejected the idea of traveling around Africa. Peace Corps volunteers were not welcomed or allowed to travel in Southern Rhodesia and South Africa. Frelimo in Mozambique was fighting the Portuguese for independence. Angola had a similar struggle. I could not get a quick visa for Rwanda. Burundi was getting over a genocide. Idi Amin was still in Uganda. By the time I finished looking over the African map, the continent seemed too dangerous or limiting.

Most of my friends traveled back the usual, shorter way through Europe, taking in Egypt, Turkey, or Israel on the way to Western Europe. One visited Somalia, another Sudan. I had already visited Israel, Egypt, and Greece.

I decided to travel around the world through Asia. My readjustment portion of about $700 got me as far as Thailand. I brought travelers cheques with me. Another $550 got me back to Wisconsin. I took in 15 countries in just less than three months. When I arrived in Hawaii, U.S. Customs showed me a list of six countries that had cholera, asking me if I had been in any of them in the past six weeks. I had been in all of them but over a period of three months. "Report to a doctor if you have any symptoms," they said, and let me go.

George related to me that, before he left Kenya, he went shopping in Nairobi at one of the outdoor curio markets. He was interested in several items but did not like the high price the vendors were asking. George knew what he thought was a fair price and knew how to bargain. The vendors turned out to be Luhyas. They assumed George was a tourist, not knowing that he had worked with Luhyas for more than three years and understood some of what they were saying. George did not let on anything about his background. The Luhyas were complaining among themselves about George's hard bargaining. "What kind of tough *mzungu* tourist is this?" they were saying in a ridiculing way. Finally, they said to George in English, "Are you going to buy or not?"

George looked at them and said, "*Tawe!*" (No, in Kiluhya) and walked away. Jaws dropping, the vendors let out a loud "*Eieee*," shocked that George may have understood their conversation.

I sent my curios and other collectibles home in several separate boxes through the postal service by slow boat to the United States. All my items eventually arrived. George bought a trunk and shipped all his items in it via another shipping service. His trunk burned in a warehouse fire in Canada.

PART VI—RECRE-ATION

CHAPTER 58—NEEDING RESPITE

One of the most interesting hitchhiking adventures during my service in Kenya was to Uganda in July of 1971. I was suffering from undiagnosed giardia and getting depressed about work. I had met two Uganda Peace Corps women at a party in Nairobi. They were both secondary teachers working in Masaka near the Rwanda border. I decided to get away from my site for a long weekend to go to see them. Two of the best things I could do to get my head together when needed were to either hit the road, if just for a couple of days, or ride around on a tractor for a few hours doing field operations, like I did on my home farm. Obviously, the tractor and farm were not available.

I succeeded in hitchhiking most of both directions. I got a ride from Eldoret to Bungoma, another to Kampala, another to Mbarara, and then took a taxi the last part to Masaka. I remember asking directions in Kampala from one of Idi Amin's soldiers on a street corner. The soldier was very friendly. It was six months into Amin's regime. The country had not yet fallen into disarray. This was my only trip to Uganda during my years in Kenya.

I spent two nights at the mission school with the Peace Corps women. Three other volunteers were there. We played cards and softball on Sunday afternoon. I felt much better, got my thoughts together, and went back to Kenya. From Jinja, I got a short ride with Ugandan Asians who were just coming from the cremation funeral of Jayant Madhvani, the Ugandan sugar magnate and richest man in East Africa. Within a year most, if not all, the Asians were expelled from Uganda by Idi Amin.

It was after dark when I found myself in Tororo near the Kenya border. I was looking for an American couple who were contract teachers living there. I located the house, but they were not home. I stood on the road for a while near the house. The couple eventually showed up and invited me for the night. The teachers had been bat-collecting near Mount Elgon. They told me there were about 25 species of bats in East Africa that they were looking for. There are more than two hundred species in Africa, including fruit bats (African Wildlife Foundation). The teachers were bat enthusiasts who were studying the creatures for a potential book project.

I returned to Eldoret the next day, hitching the last of three rides with a man wearing goggles and driving a bus chassis. I sat on the toolbox behind the driver's seat. I had renewed energy to get back to work.

I never asked the Peace Corps for permission to go to Uganda, although I did so when I went to Tanzania. I could easily have been sent home for the offense. I was not aware of or did not remember the rule but should have known better. More than once since then, I have heard of volunteers in other countries being sent home for much less. Alan Johnston told me during his review of this book that he did not recall informing the Peace Corps in Nairobi when he went on vacation to Uganda. The urgency of informing the Peace Corps about Uganda had probably increased during my service because of Idi Amin.

The Peace Corps found out about my trip and threatened me with a fine, but it never materialized. David Redgrave, the agriculture assistant director who eventually came to visit, seemed to be sympathetic to my situation. The Peace Corps was rightfully concerned for our safety. I was fortunate to have a good working relationship with Redgrave.

By our third year, George and I had a sufficiently good reputation for our extension work in western Kenya that we were asked to host the Washington Director, Donald Hess, on a field visit to Kenya. My third year in Kenya was one of the best years of my life.

I have been a lifelong advocate for the Peace Corps and have attended many of their reunions, including the 20th and 25th in Washington, D.C. I talked to many prospective volunteers. Had I been sent home I would likely have been bitter about the Peace Corps instead of being positive about it.

Had I been sent home my life would have been much different. I probably would have been drafted for Vietnam. My outlook toward the world, like many returned veterans I have met, would likely have been quite different, and probably more negative.

Had I been sent home my lifelong pursuit of international work may not have happened. I perhaps would never have returned to Kenya or to Africa. I perhaps would never have returned to see Jackson. I would surely not be writing this book.

CHAPTER 59—SALAAMA TIMES

Jackson's brother, Tom Japheth Murunga, was enrolled in a bachelor's program at the University of Dar es Salaam. Later, in 1971, with a vacation approved by the Peace Corps and an official Tanzanian visa, I decided to visit Japheth. Jackson had heard that Japheth married a Tanzanian woman there and told me to find out if it was true. I got the impression that Jackson was concerned, but I was never told why.

I took a night bus from Nairobi to Tanzania, specifically to Korogwe. There were two buses leaving at the same time. Someone said there were long waits at customs on the Tanzania border. At about midnight and nearing the border, the two buses suddenly raced to get there first. Speeding in a large passenger bus was extremely dangerous, of course. Someone said there was a single-lane bridge before the border. Sitting toward the back of the bus, I was quite upset.

We got to the bridge first. Many of the people on the bus cheered. We got to the border first. I got the name of the bus driver and planned to report him later, but never did.

The border lived up to its billing. We were delayed for two hours while Tanzanian customs agents checked luggage for imported items that were subject to duties. The agents were mostly interested in the few Asians on the bus who seemed to have a lot of taxable items. They did not bother with me.

We resumed our trip. Somewhere in the dark of night, the bus driver decided to give an old Maasai man waving along the road a free ride. Apparently, this was common practice. George mentioned the bus he took to Kilimanjaro was also picking up Maasai.

The Maasai man got on the bus wearing the usual Maasai clothing and carrying a spear. He let out a loud grunt and jammed the spear into the floor of the bus. The man appeared to be either drunk, not mentally-well, or perhaps confused. Another younger Maasai man with ear ornaments typical of the tribe and in civilian-type clothing was sitting in the front. He got up, talked to the old man in his language, took his spear, disassembled it, and gave him his seat.

The old Maasai man was not traveling far. He could not tell by looking into the night from the bus where he was. After a mile or so, he shouted for the bus to stop. The two Maasai men got off the bus to check where they were. Not yet, they decided, and got back on the bus. After another mile, they stopped again. Not yet. Another mile passed and another stop. When the men got off the third time, the bus driver drove away, leaving both behind. Everyone on the bus laughed.

It was mid-day when I arrived in Korogwe. I decided to spend the night there. There were no Peace Corps volunteers in Tanzania at the time to spend a night with. I asked if there were any other foreigners in town. "Check at the secondary school," I was told by a passerby. I found a Canadian woman, a CUSO (formerly Canadian University Services Overseas) volunteer. She said I could stay over if I promised not to try anything funny (sexual).

The woman turned out to be a reasonable but somewhat hostile host, not because I was a man, but because I was an American. A pacifist, she gave me an earful about the Vietnam War. I assured her that I was against the war, hence one of my reasons for joining the Peace Corps but, as an individual, I could not control my government. She also defended President Nyerere's brand of socialism, a system I had doubts about. I kept those opinions to myself.

The next day, I caught up with Japheth at the University of Dar es Salaam. Dar es Salaam was the Tanzanian capital at the time. The capital has since been moved to Dodoma.

I was not permitted by the university to stay in Japheth's dorm room. He kept me there anyway. There was no spare bed, but I had a sleeping bag, and the floor was comfortable.

Japheth was indeed married to a fellow student called "Apie," short for Appasiana. She was a Chaga from the Mount Kilimanjaro area of Tanzania. Apie lived at another location on campus. I saw her later again in Kisumu. They never did have children. Japheth took three other wives.

Japheth invited me to a film night at the auditorium on campus. "You are in for a real treat," he said. "They are showing a documentary, made in the Soviet Union, about the 1917 Russian Revolution." I expressed some concern about my safety as a capitalist American. "Don't worry," he replied. "Tanzanians are nice people, even if they are socialist. In fact, they are probably nicer people because of it!"

It was a silent film with English subtitles. Lenin, condemning the capitalist West and all other opponents, was at a podium shaking his fist and blowing steam from his mouth in the cold Moscow winter. The students in the auditorium cheered loudly. I was the only white person in the place and surely the only American. I crouched lower in my seat.

Japheth eventually finished his bachelor's degree from the University of Dar es Salaam. He later received a Masters' degree in

Australia in brewing and became the chief brewer at Tusker in Ruiru north of Nairobi. He gave me a tour of the plant in 1973 and met me for a beer at the Nairobi Intercontinental in 1987.

One morning, as I was standing in the doorway of my hotel in Dar es Salaam contemplating my next move, a man snatched a purse from a woman on the other side of the street. Suddenly, a group of bystanders took off in hot pursuit of the thief, throwing stones at him as he ran. The thief dropped the purse and escaped. The hotel manager came up next to me. "We Tanzanians don't tolerate such things," he said. "The thief would be lucky if the police came because he might be killed by the mob."

I booked a flight to Zanzibar just for the day. The Zanzibar and Pemba Islands were part of the federation with Tanganyika to form Tanzania. As part of the agreement, Zanzibar had one of the two vice presidents of Tanzania. At the time, it was Abeid Karume, who ruled Zanzibar with an iron fist. He was assassinated a year later (Wikipedia).

The flights over to Zanzibar and back were on DC-3s, 25-seat aircraft built in the 1930s-1940s. I was required by law to hire a tour guide for the day on Zanzibar. About half of what I saw was not allowed to be photographed, mainly government buildings. I did get to photograph the famous slave market, the house where the missionary and explorer, David Livingston, stayed when coming and going on his trips to the interior, and several ornate Arabic doors.

The Sultan of Zanzibar controlled the coast of East Africa for centuries. Livingston and other explorers needed his permission to go into the interior. There was no going into the interior north of Zanzibar because the Maasai formed an effective barrier along the future Kenya coast. By the 1890s, however, the Maasai were devastated by rinderpest, a disease that killed many of their cattle, and by syphilis, a disease that rendered many women sterile. Both diseases were brought to East Africa by Europeans. The Maasai were never again the formidable force they once were.

By 1900, the British were able to plan their railroad from Mombasa through Maasai country on to Lake Victoria. However, there were still obstacles. The railroad workers were attacked by the famous "lions of Tsavo," and then faced fierce armed resistance from the Nandis in western Kenya.

The Zanzibar slave market was probably the largest in the Indian Ocean region (Wikipedia). Run by Arabs with African collaboration in the interior for more than a thousand years, approximately 17 million slaves were sold there, often 40,000-50,000 per year. That number does not include the many slaves who died carrying ivory and other goods before they reached the coast. Some illegal slave trading continued until the British took control over the region.

CHAPTER 60—THE TEACHER

Julius K. Nyerere served as prime minister, then as president of Tanganyika, then Tanzania, from 1961 to 1985 (Wikipedia). He was born in the Lake Victoria area and was a Catholic school teacher in his early days. He was affectionately known as *"Mwalimu"* (teacher).

Nyerere was one of the few non-corrupted, or at least, less-corrupted, African leaders. He lived on his meager presidential salary. He could walk in the street without fear, greeting people as he went. When Nyerere stepped down from power in 1985, he was only the fourth post-independence African leader to voluntarily do so. By my estimate, roughly 50 post-independence African leaders had been gone by that time, almost all by military overthrow or death.

Nyerere pursued a path of socialism. He unified the country under the banner of Swahili and *"Ujamaa"* (family, familyhood). Whenever I visited Tanzania and asked any citizen what tribe he was, he would proudly say that he was a Tanzanian. Nyerere not only succeeded in unifying the country but avoided the tribalism and violence that beset most of his neighbors. Nyerere's treatise, *The Arusha Declaration,* is one of the more idealistic political statements ever written. Unfortunately, Nyerere's socialism also slowed the economy, falling far behind the more capitalistic Kenya across the border.

Nyerere wanted to avoid the Cold War politics that seemed to be dividing Africa between Western and Soviet influence. He aligned himself with Communist China.

In the early 1970s, Nyerere invited the Chinese to build a railroad to bring copper from Zambia to the port of Dar es Salaam. The Chinese did build the railway, a "narrow gauge" or 3-foot, 6-inch width to match existing railways in Zambia and most of the region. It was the largest foreign project ever done by the Chinese up to that point (Wikipedia). It allowed Zambia to avoid having to ship its copper through Southern Rhodesia and South Africa, both apartheid regimes at the time.

I saw Chinese workers in Dar es Salaam, usually moving around in groups of a half-dozen or so. I was curious to talk to them. I finally found one Chinese fellow in a restaurant and approached him.

"Wrong Chinese!" he laughed. "I'm a student from Taiwan. Those Communist Chinese guys do not speak English anyway. The Chinese government doesn't want them to communicate with foreigners," he continued. "They might defect!"

"Why don't the Chinese hire local Tanzanians?" I then asked.

"The Chinese prefer to bring their own skilled people rather than train locals," he replied. "Plus, it is income for Chinese workers. It keeps more of the Chinese foreign investment money at home."

Starting in 2017, the Tanzanian government has contracted to replace the entire system of narrow-gauge railways with the standard-gauge (Wikipedia). I have seen many Chinese projects all over Africa. They still bring many of their own workers.

CHAPTER 61—WONDERS OF AFRICA

When an opportunity comes along to see several of the wonders of Africa, literally in your back yard, you do not pass it up! Several Peace Corps volunteers, including myself, accompanied Chief Water Engineer Arthur Spore on a safari in 1972. Arthur Spore was part of the first Kenya Peace Corps group in 1964. As of 2018, I was told that he was still living in Kenya. In 1972, Spore owned a Jeep Wagoneer that held nine people.

The safari lasted nine days. The route went from Eldoret to Kericho to Sotik to Maasai Mara, then into Tanzania in Serengeti, to Ngorongoro Crater, to Olduvai Gorge, to Lake Manyara, to Arusha, to Moshi, around Kilimanjaro, back into Kenya, to Amboseli to Nairobi and back to Eldoret. We camped out the whole way.

Because we were East African residents, the game park fees were just 10 Ksh. Campsites cost extra. The Kenya-Tanzania border between Maasai Mara and Serengeti was still open at that time but has been closed for many years since. Tanzania wants tourists to enter the country and start their safaris via Arusha.

In Kericho, we stopped at the famous Tea Hotel for a drink. Kericho is the largest tea-growing area in Kenya, the home of

Brooke Bond and other tea companies. The Kenya Tea Marketing Board, unlike the Maize and Produce Board, had a good reputation at the time for efficiency and profit. One reason for its success was that the board was composed of a majority representation of producer members, and a minority of government and processor members. Marketing boards were holdovers from the colonial times, intended to provide raw commodities from the colonies to Great Britain. At the time of this writing, Kenya was the third-largest producer of tea in the world behind China and India, and just ahead of Sri Lanka (worldatlas.com).

The Maasai Mara Game Park in Kenya is the smaller, northern extension of the Serengeti plain. Spore kept a lighted Petromax kerosene lamp on top of the vehicle at night to ward off wild animals. Nonetheless, giraffes passed near our campsite before we turned in. When I got up in the middle of the night to relieve myself, I suddenly saw a cape buffalo standing near me in the shadows. The lamp may have kept animals out of the center of the camp but may also have attracted the curious onlookers on the fringe. Lions took no interest in us that night, but one male roared several times during the night, his voice echoing everywhere. No doubt he wanted to let everyone know who was boss.

Serengeti was, and still is, one of the greatest natural wonders I have ever seen. We missed the main migration in 1972 but saw every type of animal imaginable. Part of the list included wildebeests, hartebeests, zebras, kudus, bush bucks, impalas, gazelles, kongonis, elephants, rhinos, hippos, cape buffalo, wart hogs, baboons, monkeys, giraffes, ostriches, lions, cheetahs, leopards, hyenas, secretary birds, kites, and buzzards. I was fortunate to return to Serengeti again in 2006 in the middle of the migration.

There are over a million wildebeests in Serengeti. We noticed that, if they happened to be running across the road in front of our vehicle, they would nicely peel off in order not to get hit and then reform their run behind us. As dumb as they look, wildebeests are smart animals! Contrast that to our cute whitetail deer in northern Wisconsin where I live, who seem hellbent to run out into the road and die in front of our vehicles!

We came across a mother cheetah and three offspring in Serengeti. She obviously wanted to lead us away from her little ones. We took up the chase, getting up to 40 miles per hour. The cheetah just loped along. Even though we had a relatively clear view of the turf, Spore would not go any faster for fear of hitting a termite mound hidden in the grass. Such a mound could take out the bottom of the car engine.

Termite mounds can be several feet high. They feature a unique ventilation system that maintains a consistent inside temperature, no matter what the outside temperature is. The system is needed to grow a certain type of fungus within the mound that the termites consume. The Eastgate Centre office and shopping complex in Harare, Zimbabwe was designed based on termite ventilation. It needs no conventional air-conditioning or heating (Jill Fahrenbacher, inhabitat.com).

From Serengeti, we moved to Ngorongoro Crater. We needed a four-wheel-drive vehicle to descend the steep road two thousand feet into the crater. The Jeep Wagoneer was just such a vehicle. Nonetheless, we were also required to take a tour guide with us. He sat in the passenger seat in the front.

Ngorongoro provided some interesting incidents. We found a lion couple resting in the grass. They paid no attention to us. The lions just yawned, having seen thousands of tourists. After shutting off the vehicle, we opened the sunroof. Six of us stood up and verbally teased the lions to make them look at us to get a good photo. Suddenly, the male charged us, stopping just short of the guide's window. The guide was quite startled but said nothing. Those of us standing quickly retreated down into the vehicle and closed the sunroof. We left the scene.

For lunch, we stopped at a picnic site next to a small lake in the crater. There were several large brown birds sitting in the trees we guessed to be kites. Once we unpacked our sandwiches and started to eat, the birds took to the air. Suddenly, one bird dived and took a sandwich out of one person's hand. We discovered that, even if we held the sandwich close to our mouths, one bird would buzz very closely, causing the person to stretch out both hands to defend himself. A second bird close behind then took the sandwich. A piece of food thrown into the air never reached the ground.

Two of my colleagues decided to buy craft items from two Maasai vendors nearby. They negotiated in Swahili. My colleagues' Swahili was not particularly good. Maasai in Kenya were not required to go to school. Maasai in Tanzania, however, were required to attend grade school, learning both Swahili and English. Finally, the Maasai, not impressed with the Swahili they were hearing, said, "Why don't you just speak English?"

The campsite at the top of Ngorongoro was near the gravesite memorial dedicated to Michael Grzimek, aged 24, who died in a small plane crash in 1959 while studying Serengeti migrations (Wikipedia). His plane hit a large buzzard. Michael and his father Bernhard wrote the book *Serengeti Shall Not Die* and directed the movie of the same name. The Grzimeks, who were from Germany, were influential in the designation of Serengeti as a national park. Bernhard, a veterinarian by training, had a long successful career including many years at the Frankfurt Zoo. When he died in 1987, his ashes were interred next to his son.

We stopped at Olduvai Gorge where Mary Leakey discovered the fossilized skull of Zinjanthropus in 1959, the oldest known hominid at the time, and the Leatoli footprints, among many other discoveries (biography.com//mary-leakey).

After a night at Lake Manyara National Park, we circled Mount Kilimanjaro and camped in Kenya in Amboseli National Park. The view of Kilimanjaro was spectacular with its 4,000-foot snow cap on the top. It was then that I decided I would have to climb Kilimanjaro.

I later regretted not trying to get Jackson invited along on the safari. The car filled up immediately. Jackson needed to hold down the fort while we were away. Volunteers jumped at opportunities quickly, knowing that there would be few such chances in just two or three years. I naively assumed Jackson would have other opportunities or would find a way to do these trips on his own.

CHAPTER 62—LAND ON PAUSE

I saw a travel opportunity for Jackson and me. "Let's go to Mombasa and Lamu," I said to Jackson one day in 1973. Mombasa on the Kenya coast was close to 600 miles from Tongaren. Lamu Island was another 150 or so miles up the coast near Somalia. I knew both places, having lived in Mombasa during training and having traveled to Lamu once before on vacation. Jackson, like most upcountry Kenyans, had never been to the coast and had never seen the Indian Ocean.

I showed Jackson where we were going on a map of Kenya that I had in the house. This did not help him much. It appeared that Jackson had never seen a map before or certainly never used one. He could not understand where he was on it. No matter how I tried to explain it, he just got more frustrated. It was easier just to explain directions and distance, things he would understand from his perspective. Later, he did try to make sense of my world map.

It takes some training to read maps, I realized. I grew up being fascinated with maps from grade school. I thought that maps were so obvious. Then, when I traveled with my brother to New York and Washington, D.C. in 1976, asking him to navigate our route while I was driving, I quickly realized that he was not much good at reading maps, either.

"Sure," Jackson replied. "How do we go there?"

"We'll hitchhike as far as we can, of course," I replied. "Otherwise we can take a bus or taxi. We'll be gone about a week."

I applied for some leave and Jackson made his arrangements with his family in Lumakanda to be away. Two weeks later, we hit the road, Jackson with a carry bag and me with my backpack.

We drove to Eldoret, left the Moke at Dan Dunn's house, and walked out to the highway. I had hitched from Eldoret many times before. A single white man had no trouble getting a ride. Having Jackson with me ruled out a single-seat opportunity. It also added a black person to the equation. I was not sure what was going to happen.

Jackson and I reached Nairobi, two hundred miles away, in a day with four rides, without any problem. More than the usual number of cars passed us by. However, on two occasions, the driver drove by, considered what he was looking at, turned around, and came back to get us. Both were white, and both were very curious to find out what we were up to. They had never seen a white and a black person hitchhiking together.

We got off at Westlands on the edge of Nairobi and walked to David and Fritzi Redgrave's house. The Redgraves were always receptive to Peace Corps volunteers staying at their house, whether they had space or not. They had six young children besides, three of them adopted Native Americans.

At Christmas time, many of us often gathered at the Redgraves', sleeping on sofas and the floor. It was the one time of year when some volunteers called home to the United States on the Redgraves' phone.

At the first Christmas party at the Redgraves' in 1970, I happened to be talking about an experience on my family dairy farm back home in Wisconsin. I mentioned driving a tractor. One of the other volunteers in the room commented that I did not seem like the farmer type. I was surprised. "I am an agriculture volunteer," I replied. "I come from a dairy farm. What is a farm boy supposed to look or act like?" I asked.

It made me wonder if my shy, bookish nature somehow overshadowed what was expected to be my perhaps "brusquer" farmer nature? I resented the expectation some people had about how a farmer should behave. I have noticed over my lifetime that, unless I bring up my agriculture background, people do not see that in me. Interesting!

David Redgrave was, in my opinion, the quintessential Peace Corps staff person. A big fellow with a red beard and a PhD in soils from Montana, his patience and welcoming nature helped volunteers over some humps and made my experience so much better. The Redgraves heartily welcomed Jackson and me. They were quite interested in hearing about our adventure.

The next day, Jackson and I got back out on the highway toward Mombasa. We were able to get a ride as far as Mtito Andei, more than halfway to Mombasa. From noon until about 3:00 p.m., we were stranded. Part of the reason for the delay was an elephant standing on the highway just outside of the village. Mtito Andei is in the middle of the east and west divisions of the Tsavo Game Park. Jackson had never seen an elephant before.

Finally, with the elephant having left, a car stopped with room for one. I told Jackson to get in and told the driver to drop him off at the main market in Mombasa. After waiting another half hour, I decided to take a country taxi.

After locating Jackson at the market, we took the local Bamburi bus up the north shore to Kisauni. I had written to my former Swahili training host there, Mohammed Salim Ahmed. He was expecting us. We stayed there for the night and were treated to a good meal and conversation.

The next day, we boarded the bus for Lamu. There were the usual stops at Kilifi and Malindi. Two young French tourists tried to board the bus at Malindi without having purchased tickets in advance. There was no room. They refused to get off. They did not speak much English. The ticket collector asked me to intercede. "You are white person," he said. "Maybe they will listen to you." Before I could say anything, they got off.

From Malindi, it was a long, dusty ride to the port across from Lamu. The loud Arabic music on the bus was oppressive. We had to cross the Tana River by ferry. The ferry was pulled across the river by men from the bus pulling on a rope. Jackson and I assisted.

At the port, we boarded a small motorboat. After loading, the boat was only about three inches above the waterline. Jackson was rather nervous. He mentioned that he could not swim. I told him not to worry, my ability to swim was not good either! After about 20 minutes, we arrived in Lamu.

Lamu village had very narrow streets with many donkeys. There was only one car on the entire island. It belonged to the district commissioner (DC). Lamu was a small island with only a few roads. There was hardly anywhere to drive the car. The buildings were quite old. Lamu looked like time had stood still.

If you needed to change traveler's cheques, Barclays Bank was the only bank in town. The sign next to the door stated, "Hours of Business, Second and Last Wednesday of Each Month, 10:00-12:00 and 2:00-3:00."

"Typical bankers' hours," I thought to myself. In a pinch, the DC's office could change your cheques.

I located the cheap, hippie hotel I had stayed at the first time I came. There was one big room with at least a dozen cots. Jackson and I staked out our places. There were several young European travelers in the room. Suddenly, one of them objected to Jackson being in room. I was shocked, not expecting Jackson to be the subject of racism in such a place.

Jackson said nothing. I quickly formulated a response in his defense but, before I could say anything, one of the other Europeans spoke up. "This is his continent and his country!" he said of Jackson. "He has every right to be here and is obviously a friend of this gentleman," he said, pointing to me. "We are the guests here!" Nothing more was said.

The next day we spent several hours in the ocean. I got the worst sunburn of my life. Even Jackson complained of sunburn. We spent three days on the island. Jackson and I talked about the culture of the coast, especially the Arab and Muslim influences.

The trip an eye-opening experience for Jackson, and a wonderful time for the two of us to enjoy travel and recreation together. Two of Jackson's daughters would later work in hotels on the coast, and he would return to visit them.

CHAPTER 63—FOOTBALL
WITHOUT PADS

In 1972, George and I were approached to join the Eldoret rugby team. They were short of players. After I explained that I had no formal sports experience, not even in high school, I was told that my height, at 6 feet, 1/2-inch, would be a good fit for a position in the line-out. Surprisingly, as I write this book in my early 70s, I am now 6 feet, 3/4-inch tall, attributing my gain in height to four years of weekly yoga classes.

I was also touted by the rugby team to be big and strong enough for the second line of the scrum. George got a similar request. He and I crouched side by side in the scrum, he on the right and me on the left. It was disgusting for me to stick my head between ugly, hairy, sweaty men's legs, but that was part of the game! Bob Nusbaum ended up in the front line of the scrum. He had been a high school football player and served as a place kicker for the rugby team. David Johnson also played. One urban volunteer in our Peace Corps group played for a Nairobi team.

A notable fellow named Robinson, from Ireland, was a skilled player on the Eldoret team. He told me in the bar after one game that he was a member of the Irish Republican Army. Robinson said that he took a job in Kenya to get away from the heat (tensions) back home.

Two of our Dutch friends played on the team. Three Kenyans, lanky and fast, were recruited for the wing positions.

I was not fit for rugby. The first couple of games left me very winded. Playing at 5,000-6,000 feet did not help. I briefly took up running to get into shape, doing about five miles one way and then walking back. Small Kenyan boys ran with me, taking three strides for every one of mine, yet never seemed to get tired.

The Eldoret rugby team had a bad year. There were 12 games, but we only won two. There was Thika, the team that won the championship, Mount Kenya, Nakuru, and three teams in Nairobi, the Nondescripts, Harlequins, and Impalas. It was in the Nondescripts game in Nairobi that I suffered the one and only concussion in my life. I remember a collision and then seeing stars. I was pulled from the game. Rugby is a rough game, like American football without any padding. It is much rougher if you do not know how to play it correctly.

The camaraderie after the games in the bar with drinking and dancing was the best part. After the game in Thika, I remember two very sexy women dancing to the T. Rex song "Get It On." John Davis, a British friend at the Ministry of Agriculture, played for Thika.

Dennis Syth, our Peace Corps Wisconsin colleague in Nyeri, played two seasons for the Mount Kenya team. After our win against them on their home turf, an older British woman named Ada came up to Dennis and said with a smile, "Why can't you *blokes* (characters, idiots) get your *bloody* (damned) thumbs out for just one game?" I was never quite sure where she thought the thumbs would have been.

While we were in Nyeri, we spotted a rough-looking man with long, knotted hair and a beard wearing animal skins. I asked Syth about it. He said that there were a few Mau Mau fighters still hiding out in the nearby forests who occasionally emerged. They seemed not to know or accept that the Mau Mau Rebellion ended ten years before.

George and I only played rugby that one year. Rugby eventually got me into reasonable shape, something useful for two climbs up Kilimanjaro in 1973. Eldoret would win the championship in the next year or two.

CHAPTER 64—BACKYARD MONOLITH

M ount Elgon was a special mountain for me. Only about thirty miles from Tongaren, it loomed large over my settlement area. I spent many moments pondering its massive existence. Nearby towns like Kitale, Endebess, and Kimilili were all in the foothills.

Elgon, an extinct volcano, straddles the Kenya-Uganda border. The highest point is 14,177 feet, which lies on the Uganda side. It is the 17th highest mountain in Africa (Uganda Wildlife Authority, Wikipedia). Unlike Mount Kilimanjaro and Mount Kenya, Elgon is not high enough to accumulate snow. It is 50 miles across at the base, making it the widest volcano in the world. By comparison, Kilimanjaro, made up of three peaks, is a mere 40 miles wide! Elgon is the oldest volcano in East Africa and was once believed to have towered well over 20,000 feet.

Elgon is famous for its Kitum Cave, which extends 700 feet into the side of the mountain (Wikipedia). There is a herd of elephants and other wild species on the mountain that go into the cave to take advantage of the salt deposits there. The cave is also home to thousands of fruit bats and insect-eating bats (*The Hot Zone*, book by

Richard Preston). I heard that the Elgon bats consumed up to four tons of insects each night. We owe a lot to bats. How many mosquitoes, for instance, does it take to make a ton?

Several of us Peace Corps volunteers climbed Elgon in 1971 with a few of our Dutch volunteer friends. There was no special tourist route at the time. We drove two Mokes and two Land Rovers as far up the mountain as we could, camped out at the edge of the tree line (10,000 feet), and climbed the next day.

We reached the edge of the crater in a few hours. The huge crater, containing mostly grassy vegetation, was close to ten miles across. Down in the bottom of the crater, in the middle, was a small African house. The man who lived there eventually came up, greeted us, and said he was going down the Kenya side to do some shopping. Technically, the entire mountain top is a game park.

I asked the man which country he lived in. "I do not know,'" he replied, "and I do not care. No one bothers me; no one ever comes to my house. No land cost, no taxes. I like it that way."

Climbing a mountain like Elgon without a trail is easy because you just head for the peak. Once up there, however, the mountain looks much the same downhill, no matter which direction you look. One volunteer we met later said that he was forced to spend an extra night on the mountain because he got lost coming down.

While we were at the top, we noticed some reflections from our campsite. Someone was opening a vehicle door, it seemed. When we returned to the campsite, we found that thieves had taken some of our belongings, including the Dutch tents. Fortunately, we had our camera equipment with us. Nonetheless, the Dutch figured they had lost about $600 worth of items. The vehicles were not taken. I lost a sleeping bag and suitcase. It was the same suitcase that my parents took on their honeymoon in 1946.

CHAPTER 65—SNOW ON THE EQUATOR

L ater in 1971, several of us who had climbed Elgon decided to tackle Mount Kenya, the second-highest mountain in Africa after Kilimanjaro. Mount Kenya lies almost on the equator. There is a point in the Ngong Hills in Nairobi where one can see both mountains on a clear day.

Because of our restrictions on the use of the Mokes, we rode with the Dutch. Mount Kenya, called "Kirinyaga" by the native Kikuyus in the area, was 300 miles from Eldoret via Nairobi. According to Kikuyu tradition, Kirinyaga is where God first introduced Kikuyus to the earth (*Facing Mount Kenya,* book by Jomo Kenyatta).

We spent two nights on the mountain at the same hut, once going up and once coming down. My sleeping bag was thin and the hut so cold that I could hardly sleep, even though I also wore all the clothes I had with me.

We reached Point Lenana, the highest safe peak, at 16,355 feet. There is a metal cross positioned here. There are two higher peaks that require specialized climbing equipment, the highest being 17,057 feet. We heard later that two volunteers we did not know had scaled the two highest peaks without equipment. Another time, a rescue helicopter crashed near the high peak trying to rescue a climber with a broken leg, killing the chopper crew.

CHAPTER 66—ABOVE THE CLOUDS

Kilimanjaro is the tallest mountain in Africa at 19,341 feet and the tallest free-standing mountain in the world (Wikipedia). The surrounding area lies at an elevation of about 3,000 feet. The park entrance starts at 6,000 feet. Below that, there are forests and farmland. Kilimanjaro is made up of three peaks (volcanic cones), two of which are considered extinct. Kibo, the highest peak, is considered dormant, having erupted about 150,000 years ago. Transpiration from the base contributes to the snowfall and glaciers on the top. The mountain has not been active, nor has it been heating up. The disappearance of the glaciers and famous snowcap on Kilimanjaro in recent times has been largely attributed to climate change.

Seven volunteers from Wisconsin climbed Kilimanjaro in March 1973, including George Roemer, Dan Dunn, Jim Orf, David Johnson, Bob Nusbaum, and me. One of the Dutch volunteers, Huub Lamers, also went along. We took the Marangu tourist route, a well-beaten and busy path, to the top. Nonetheless, we were required to hire a guide whether we needed one or not. Having a guide turned out to be a good idea. We learned a lot about the mountain and about how to pace ourselves. "*Pole, pole!*" he kept saying. "Go slow, do not rush."

We added one porter to carry food and cooking supplies. The small propane canisters we used for cooking were not available in Tanzania, so we had to bring them from Kenya. Each of us carried our own backpack with personal items and additional food. My pack probably weighed 20-25 pounds. A few colleagues rented hiking boots and soon complained about blisters. George said he lost two toenails. I wore my soft, everyday safari shoes and got only a few blisters. The total cost of the climb for each of us was about $125.

The Marangu route was about 40 miles to the top, a five-day trip up and down. The climb was not really a climb, but rather a long walk. We were all in our mid-twenties, living at 5,000-6,000 feet. Five of us had played rugby. Being fit for Kilimanjaro is important. Acclimating, adapting to the altitude, is most important. Many people get headaches at high altitudes. I did not, but my stomach was often queasy.

The Mandara Hut at 9,500 feet was our destination on the first day. It was still below the tree line, which was 10,000 feet. The capacity there was about 50 persons. Some climbers coming back down would stay at either the second or first hut. Mandara was rather luxurious compared to the other two huts. There were two large rooms that had individual beds with mattresses. It even had a fireplace. This hut was accessible for supplies by Land Rover via a rough road.

Our supply of carbs was mostly rice with some jam and other sweets. At higher altitudes, the rice did not cook well. Fortunately, there were two Japanese tourists with us who could cook rice anywhere, perhaps even on the moon! They were short of rice and we had plenty, so they cooked in exchange for some of our cache. Our protein supply was spam, beans, nuts, and dried beef.

The vegetative zones of Kilimanjaro went from agriculture at the base to tropical rainforest to moorland to alpine desert to stone desert to what was considered eternal ice at the time (Wikipedia). Grasses, ferns, mosses, and imposing-looking giant groundsels dominated the moorland zone.

The second hut, Horombo, consisted of two metal shacks with wooden bunks. There were no trees at 15,000 feet. In fact, there was little vegetation at all. The cold wind coming up the side of the mountain was bone-chilling. We could see down to the bottom of the mountain for a short part of the day. Generally, we were either in the clouds or above the clouds. The capacity of this hut was about 35-40.

From the second hut to the third hut, one crosses a saddle between the two older peaks and the huge snow-capped crater. The saddle is a pure rocky desert. The third hut, Kibo, at 15,500 feet, was like the second one, just a couple of metal shacks. The capacity was about 25, which basically determined the maximum climb for the day. Not everyone who climbed reached this hut.

The climb to the top began at midnight from Kibo Hut. The idea was to reach 18,600 feet by sunrise six hours later to enjoy the view over Mawenzi, the older, smaller extinct peak. This part of the venture was a series of switchbacks up a gravelly scree.

We reached the 18,600-foot rim as scheduled. My colleagues voted to go back down from there. I wanted to walk another mile or less to the high point, 19,341 feet, but I had to stick with the group. We skied on our feet back down the scree part. What took us six miserable hours to traverse upward took about 15 minutes to go down. It is incredible how the altitude issues go away immediately once one starts heading down.

Not wanting to spend another night at the second hut, we continued to the first hut. I almost never drank beer in my youth. However, when we reached the end of our climb, we all had a cold one at the Marangu Lodge near the gate.

The unsubstantiated and probably untrue story is that Kilimanjaro used to be in Kenya, a British colony, but ended up in Tanganyika, a German colony at the time. Queen Victoria allegedly gave it to her nephew, the German Kaiser Wilhelm II, as a birthday present (*Kenya Africa Nation,* July 14, 2013). There is, after all, a distinct bend in the border that appears as if the border had been moved. However, earlier attempts to make a straight border from the coast to Lake Victoria found Kilimanjaro to be in the way. Some versions of a proposed border may have cut the mountain in two. Dividing the mountain would not necessarily have been unique, because Kenya and Uganda did split Mount Elgon. More likely, Kilimanjaro was involved in a trade that gave Mombasa and Zanzibar to the British. The mountain was not moved, but the final border was!

I climbed Kilimanjaro for a second time in 1973 in December. A very athletic Scotsman went with me, so we shared the guide. For the much of the climb, the Scot ran ahead of me.

Once above the tree line, I spied a small herd of eland near a small lake. I did not anticipate finding such wildlife at that altitude. But then, Ernest Hemingway in 1936 did not expect to find the carcass of a leopard at 18,000 feet either (*The Snows of Kilimanjaro*).

I met three Europeans in the saddle having lunch. They told me they were going straight through from bottom to top and back without spending a night. They figured it would take about 18 hours. Nothing like being in really good shape!

An older guide at Kibo, who also guided on Mawenzi, told us over his campfire that a few people had died on Mawenzi over the years. Two or more bodies were never recovered. Climbing Mawenzi demanded special equipment. "There once were two climbers tied together with a rope," he said. "One fell forward into a crevasse and the other fell backward off a cliff. Both died dangling in the air. We were able to recover the body on this side by shooting the rope off with a rifle."

On the last part, what took me the normal six hours, for the Scot took four hours. My singular goal was to get to the very top. Even though my stomach was off on the last part and I vomited a few times, I did not quit. The guide told me to turn around. I refused.

This time, when I got to the rim, I walked the extra 45 minutes to the highest point. I had no sunglasses, so the glare of the sun on the glacier blinded me for much of the last part. At the very top, 19,341 feet, was a small cross with a pencil and sign-in book in a box. Pens do not write at freezing temperatures on mountain tops. I signed the book with the pencil, but never went to get a certificate from the climbing office when I got back to Arusha. This climb cost me $50.

In 2006, I attempted the mountain for the third time, stopping at the Kibo hut. I was going on 58 and more than a bit out of shape. I thought it was not worth risking a heart attack when I had already been at the top twice before. A month later, a fellow Kiel High School graduate like myself and four years older than me, died of a heart attack on the final ascent.

Chapter 67—Fishing for Souls, Not Crocodiles

I took a final week of vacation to go to Lodwar near Lake Turkana, formerly known as Lake Rudolph, at the end of 1973. I had never been farther north in Kenya than Kitale. The road to Lodwar went through Kitale. I had no contacts in Lodwar. I did not know how I would go the 25 or so miles from there to the lake itself or where I would stay at any point. As usual, figured that out along the way.

Other than a private car, the only way to Lodwar was on the fish lorry. I booked a one-way trip. The lorry left in the late afternoon. It would be about an 11-hour ride.

I was the only white person on the trip. Although I offered to stand or sit on the back, the driver insisted I sit in the cab. A woman sat between us. Most of the riders on the back were young men with a few young wives and children. The lorry picked up a few more riders along the way, all men.

We stopped in Kapenguria for a brief break. Kapenguria was on the edge of an escarpment. The tarmac ended there. As we headed downward on the narrow, winding dirt road, I could see the wrecks of several trucks below. Was this a veritable "Highway to Hell" like the one in Bolivia (www.themanual.com/travel/most-dangerous-roads)? Well, not quite. But given the wrecks and the reputation of Kenyan truck drivers, I was still concerned.

For the first time in Kenya, I saw primitive naked men. Three of them were running near the road carrying spears. I was taken aback.

The road passed briefly through the edge of Uganda. Ugandan soldiers were driving around in topless vehicles that looked like Jeeps. They paid no attention to us. I was a bit nervous, nonetheless, and remained so until we arrived safely back in Kenya. Idi Amin was well into his reign of terror by that time.

The landscape was mostly flat and dry. It was now dark with a full moon. The temperature became cold. Several hours passed.

We suddenly found ourselves going down a steep hill. Another lorry was coming up the hill. The two lorries stopped face to face. The drivers got out and started arguing. It was obvious to me that the road was more than wide enough for both lorries to pass.

After some time, the arguing stopped, the drivers got back in, backed up, and moved toward opposite sides of the road, but not enough to pass. They got out once more and argued. They then moved again more to the opposite sides but, again, not enough. The drivers got out and agued again. Finally, after about 20 minutes of what I considered to be humorous nonsense, the drivers moved over enough to pass by each other, and we were on our way. I had never seen Kenyans act this way.

We arrived in Lodwar as the sun was coming up. I found a small hotel and checked in, taking a shower, breakfast, and a short nap. The temperature became quite hot, probably about 95 degrees Fahrenheit. The whole place was dry and dusty. I saw topless women sitting under a tree.

Lodwar is located roughly a half hour by road west of the lake. "I am not going to stay in this hot, rather desolate town any longer than necessary," I thought to myself. I inquired about getting transport to the lake, not knowing where I was going to end up. Fergusons Gulf on the southern shore featured a tourist resort I had heard about. I considered going there, if necessary.

I was told there was a Catholic mission on the lake. The church maintained a repair shop for their vehicles in Lodwar. An Irish priest, also working as a mechanic, was present. He told me that a parish priest and nun were taking a Land Rover to the lake in the afternoon. He said he would talk to them. "I think they will be happy to put you up for a couple of days," he said. "We do not get many visitors."

"Sure, we will take you along," the priest and nun both said. "Welcome to Turkana country!" When we reached the shore, the priest got off at a church for a service there. It was a small, mud-thatch building. I could hear people singing inside. The priest made a comment about how this small church could not hold the enthusiastic throngs of people wanting to attend while the huge cathedrals in Europe could barely attract a few dozen faithful. "We have no pipe organ, just drums, and they sing like angels!" he explained.

"You'll be going to my parsonage about 15 miles north up the shore. I'll be there in a few days," he said. "The sister here will take you there. I have a cook, plenty of food and lots of reading material. Make yourself at home!" I was really beginning to like this priest.

The nun took the wheel, driving like a race car driver on the sand along the shore. She mentioned that she lived near the parsonage in another house and ran a clinic. There was a small village with another church nearby.

"I'll instruct the cook to take good care of you but, if anything comes up, just ask for me." When we arrived, she gave instructions to the cook in his native Turkana. Then she addressed me. "He speaks Swahili and a bit of English."

"Feel free to go swimming in the lake. The crocodiles live on the other side," the nun assured me. "Swim in the morning. The local fishermen arrive with their nets later in the afternoon."

I settled in, spending three days to myself. The cook provided breakfast, told me where to find lunch, and then cooked dinner. He disappeared most of the rest of the time, stating he also had to cook for others in the parish. I had no swimwear, so went skinny-dipping two mornings. There was no one around.

It was so incredibly peaceful at Lake Turkana that no matter how hard I tried to be concerned about anything, I could not. There were but a few places in my life, high up on Kilimanjaro being another, where the remoteness, altitude, wind, waves or immense quiet of the place so completely overwhelmed my soul, imposing a kind of peace I could not fight off. In such places, nature was stronger than the man-made pollutants of the modern world like traffic, industry, smog, chemical smells, television, radio, and just plain artificial noise.

I read two books from the priest's library, one on comparative religion and one on Islam. I went out to watch the fishermen cast their nets in the evening. The fishermen and the little boys who came to check me out wore no clothes.

On the fourth day, the priest arrived by Land Rover at about the same time as the Flying Doctor Service landed a plane on a dirt runway on the shore. A patient needed to be medivacked from the village. A Danish tourist, an artist by trade, hitched in with the Service. Villagers suddenly showed up to gaze at the plane, perhaps seeing such a machine for the first time.

The artist likewise arranged to stay with the priest. That evening at the shore, the artist penciled on note paper several images of the fishermen and the boys. He gave the drawings to the boys. They were delighted!

After dinner and a beer, the priest, the artist, and I talked late into the night for two consecutive days. The priest expressed concern about the effect of his mission work on the local community. "We are, unfortunately, dividing the community," he stated. There was a small river splitting the area. "The Anglicans have a clinic, school and a church on one side. We have a clinic, school, and church on the other side. Relatives are arguing with each other over minute differences in theology," the priest bemoaned.

"This is not what God would want and this is not what I came to Africa for," he continued. "Sometimes, saving souls does more damage than good. I have contemplated going back to Ireland but, at the same time, I love these people and want to continue helping them."

I was a Lutheran. I surmised that the Danish artist was also brought up Lutheran. The discussion felt like we two Lutherans were taking a confession from a Catholic priest!

I do not know what happened to the priest after I left. I returned to Kitale again by night, riding on the back of the lorry this time, contemplating what I had experienced. I thought about the three books I had read by Colin Turnbull, the British anthropologist. These were *The Forest People*, *The Mountain People*, and *The Lonely African*, a work that particularly addressed some of the issues in Lodwar. I telephoned Turnbull after I returned to the United States, thanking him for his insights.

PART VII—AFTER-MATH

Chapter 68—Checkmating A Bishop

I need to add one more alleged Kenyan assassination to the list. I am sorry, but I literally stumbled into this one. In October 1990, I traveled to Kenya from Ethiopia on my way back to Wisconsin. I had finished the field work for my master's research at the International Livestock Centre for Africa (ILCA) in Ethiopia. My ruminant nutrition research involved tropical forage trees, so I took the opportunity to visit the International Centre for Research in Agroforestry or ICRAF outside of Nairobi. I then rented a car and drove to western Kenya to visit Jackson.

Jackson was agitated by yet another alleged assassination, nearly in Jackson's backyard, this time that of Anglican Bishop Alexander Muge from Eldoret. Muge was traveling in a car from Busia near the Ugandan border back to Eldoret (Wikipedia). The car was hit by a milk truck on the Uganda Highway, just up the road from Kipkarren River Village and within view of Jackson's farm.

The reports said that Muge died immediately (Wikipedia). The bishop was an outspoken critic of President Daniel arap Moi. He was warned by one of Moi's people to cease his criticism, limit his movements, and especially not to make the trip to Busia. I had read about the accident but was not familiar with who Muge was until I learned about his death. The accident occurred just a week before I arrived.

Jackson asked me to drive him out to the location. The tire marks from the accident were still on the highway. We walked around for several minutes as Jackson described the scene for me, pointing in several directions.

Jackson relayed that after he heard the crash and saw that there had been an accident, he ran out to the highway. The highway was blocked. Besides the involved vehicles, several passing cars were on the scene. The police quickly arrived. Jackson soon discovered that it was Muge who was in the accident and injured.

Jackson thought Muge was still alive, but that the police delayed calling for help. "They just stood around," Jackson said. "No one seemed to be giving any medical assistance to Muge." Jackson's opinion was that there obviously were orders to the police to make sure that Muge did not survive. He told me that he was quite angry with the police but vented his frustration only with other onlookers. "I didn't want to be arrested myself," Jackson said.

The death of Muge in a later report was generally considered to be a political murder ordered from Nairobi (*Kenya Daily Nation*, Sept. 18, 2010).

CHAPTER 69—REFLECTIONS FROM AFAR

I am writing this book 50 years after I first arrived in Kenya. Although I think my memory is still quite good, I am fortunate to be able to supplement it with the many photos and documents I saved. I am writing this book at a rather difficult time in the shadow of the Covid-19 pandemic of 2020. The pandemic kept me at home much of the time and more distant from several of my otherwise common social distractions.

I have been in constant touch with George and Sue Roemer, with whom I spent so much time in Kenya. I have also been in touch with Alice Murunga Shihundu, Jackson's youngest sister who is a nurse in Nairobi, and more recently, former Kenya volunteers Alan Johnston, Peter Petges, Charles Pike, and Kristine Karsteadt, my first cousin.

My Peace Corps experience in Kenya was one of the best things I have ever done, essentially setting the tone for much of the rest of my life. Most volunteers, no matter where they served, would say the same thing.

My agriculture extension job in Kenya was my first full-time position and where I discovered that I liked extension work. It was a good fit for me. Visiting farms was much more fun than sitting in an office or working in a lab. I liked the intrigue and challenge of solving farm-related problems. Of course, I liked having a salaried position with a guaranteed paycheck, even if it was not the best-paying position. I finished my career with 13 years of extension with the University of Wisconsin. My first and last were the best jobs I ever had.

Farmers are really the same everywhere. I also realized that 95% of people in the world want the same things—peace, security, home, family, food, wealth, happiness, jobs, long lives. Anybody who tells you differently has not traveled.

CHAPTER 70—HARD LANDINGS

The Peace Corps in 1970 spent three months preparing volunteers for their new country yet spent virtually no time preparing volunteers to go back home when their tours were finished. The same could be said for returning military personnel, missionaries, or people being let out of prison.

After almost four years away, I found adjusting to life back in the United States to be difficult. It was a type of post-traumatic stress. I slept on the living room floor for three weeks because the bed was too soft, and the bedroom, although not small, felt claustrophobic. There was just too much clutter everywhere. I was no longer used to having a lot of "stuff."

I needed to talk to people who understood me or were at least willing to listen but could find very few. I thought about Marco Polo coming back from his great adventure with no one to talk to or understand him. Even when I was on home leave for three weeks in the middle of my tour, the United States was a strange reality. I could not wait to get back to Kenya.

In the end, having a farm to return to was certainly better than being stuck in the suburbs. There was always plenty of work to do.

My advice for returning volunteers has been to get into graduate school as soon as possible, where you can quickly shift gears mentally and be around international people you can relate to.

After a stint in the Peace Corps, one's outlook has changed, one's standards have changed. I expected myself to be more tolerant, which was probably true of things I felt were different. But I found myself less tolerant of people whom I perceived to be not as tolerant as I thought I was.

I was frequently disgusted by the petty things that Americans thought important, like home décor or whether someone's clothes were slightly out of style. In fact, most house décor and clothing styles in the United States were incredibly bland and boring compared to those in Africa. I now often wear an African *dashiki* shirt to help liven up special occasions. I could not understand the need to drive 100 miles to go to a party for a few hours or, when a brick was left on a sidewalk, someone was likely to stumble on it and call a lawyer. Or why we needed 25 different kinds of laundry detergent when one good old box of Omo would do it.

I felt that I had spent a few years in a less-developed country only to find that my country was in many ways less-developed. I had lived with some of the poorest of the poor who led fulfilling lives only to find that my richer American relatives were leading unfulfilled lives in a sea of crass commercialism.

"Where is the most dangerous place you have ever been?" I have been asked several times by people expecting me to name some foreign country.

My answer has usually been, "I can tell you that, of the ten most dangerous places I have ever been, eight of them have been large U.S. cities. America is just another type of jungle!"

When I stood in front of the White House with my future first wife, an Ethiopian, in 1991, we saw a homeless woman digging in a trash can for food.

"Shame on America!" my fiancée shouted. "We Ethiopians have many poor people but few resources. American is rich. You have the ability and resources to prevent this. Why don't you do it?"

I was bothered when someone would not invite me to visit or stay for the night because their house was a little less than tidy, or they did not have a spare bedroom. I was bothered when someone would tell me, "You just can't drop in on them; they are so busy!" Peace Corps people are good at "crashing" pretty much anywhere. The value of the visit, the good conversation, greatly outweighs any consideration of material comforts.

People in the United States find so many excuses to avoid trying something different. Too many conversations have no depth for me. Too many things need to be black and white to be understood. Even with all the information and amenities available, many Americans live in such small worlds. What I felt the Peace Corps experience did for me was to put things into perspective, to sort the more important things in life from the not so important.

On at least three occasions in later years, foreigners living in the United States told me that I was the most international American they had ever met. That is wonderful, because it says a lot about what I have been trying to accomplish! That is also tragic, because there should be many, many more Americans who have a better level of international understanding.

I became a firm believer in an alternative national youth service. Americans need to get off their 40 acres for a year or two. If not college or military or Peace Corps, why not work in a national park or in an inner city or on a ranch? And Americans should learn another language.

CHAPTER 71—DESPERATION RETURN

When the movie "Out of Africa" came out in 1985, I became very homesick for Kenya. I bought the video of the movie. I fell in love with Karen Dinesen (1885-1962), aka Karen von Blixen (her married name) and Isak Dinesen (her pen name), played by Meryl Streep in the movie.

I watched Dr. Ali Mazrui's renowned and controversial public TV series entitled *The Africans: A Triple Heritage* in the mid-1980s (Wikipedia). The series pointed out many of the negative effects of the colonial influence and the failures of current African governments. No stone was left unturned by Mazrui. He pointed the finger of blame at everyone that he felt deserved it. Mazrui was born in Mombasa, Kenya. He taught at the University of Binghamton in New York and the University of Michigan.

As a small dairy farmer, I could not come up with the cash to visit Kenya. My decision to sell my cows in 1987 was based in part on my missing Kenya and not having opportunities to travel internationally. After the sale, one of the first things I did was buy a ticket to Kenya. It had been a long 13 years since I left.

I also used some of the cash from the sale to finance my return to the University of Wisconsin in Madison in 1988 for graduate school. I decided that having another advanced degree or two could open opportunities to pursue future international work. It did.

When I arrived at the airport in Nairobi in 1987 and was waiting for my luggage at the carousel, I saw Mazrui standing across from me. "You are Ali Mazrui," I said, introducing myself and briefly explaining my Kenya experience. "I saw your entire series on television," I told him.

"How did you like it?" he asked.

"I loved it," I said. "You certainly gave credit where credit was due!" I laughed.

"Most African governments now hate me!" he smiled. "Even my own government considers me *persona non grata*."

I rented a car and visited Jackson, Peter Wamalwa, and Tongaren Village. I visited Karen Dinesen's museum house in Nairobi.

I took the night train to Mombasa to visit Mohamed Salim Ahmed. The 10:00 p.m. Mombasa train left Nairobi after midnight. "Well, some things never change," I thought. Another thing that had not changed was the old steam locomotive of yesteryear that crawled along at 25 miles per hour. The cars rocked gently, making a click-clack noise. Because the train was late, I got a spectacular view of Kilimanjaro just as the sun was coming up. I was surprised to hear the song "Louisiana Saturday Night" by Alabama blaring over the PA system when we arrived at the Mombasa station.

When I mentioned Mazrui to Salim, he said, "Oh, you met my famous uncle! I did not know he was back in Kenya. I will have to catch up with him when he arrives in Mombasa." Salim informed me that my other training host from 1970, Al'min Muhsin, had died.

I have been back to Kenya several times since 1987, including in 1990, 1992, 1996, 2006, 2013, and 2016. I consider it my second home. My Swahili starts coming back when I return. I impress

Kenyans with my stories of the past. After all, I lived in Kenya be-fore most of them were born. It is always flattering when Kenyans tell me to stay, buy a plot of land and settle in. "You are one of us," they often say.

When Jackson and I returned to Tongaren in 1987, half of my mud house had been removed. I was told that termites had destroyed part of the roof. A watchman employed by the district officer was living there. I did not meet him at the time but would incredibly meet him in 2016 in Kapsabet. I saw the mud house again in 1990.

George and I did a Farmer-to-Farmer project in Kenya in 2013, spending a week in western Kenya taking Jackson and his son Richard around. We went to our former respective homes and offices in Lumakanda, Hoey's Bridge, Tongaren and Soy. We traveled to Eldoret, Kitale, Kakamega and Kisumu.

Bettington was no longer there. There was a pile of broken bricks. The current landowner had recycled the salvageable bricks into a new house for himself. George and I grabbed a few of the remaining brick chips for our collection. My office in Tongaren was still there and still used as an office by the county officials. The mud house was no longer there. The last of it was removed before 2006. George and Sue's house in Soy was there, but no longer occupied and deteriorating. Bob Sherwood's house on Jackson's farm had been destroyed by termites. Peter Petges's house had burned down. The Soy Club was being restored by an Asian owner.

When I first arrived in 1970, Kenya had about 11 million peo-ple. Today, the population is about 50 million. For several years, the population grew at more than four percent per year, one of the fastest rates in the world. Nairobi has grown immensely. Parts of it, espe-cially the downtown and the Karen suburban area, are as modern as Europe.

Unfortunately, Nairobi after dark now belongs to the thieves.

Many of the tourists stay in the outlying areas, not in the downtown. If they do stay downtown, they are not seen on the streets. When my wife, a friend, and I visited Kenya in 2006, we walked from our hotel near Jevanjee Gardens to the 1998 Nairobi Embassy Bombing Memorial at 5:00 p.m. on a weekday. The walk was about two miles each way. We passed by the New Stanley Hotel and the Hilton, encountering a few thousand people coming from work or shopping, and hundreds of cars. During the hour or more we took for the walk and memorial visit, we saw no other white people.

CHAPTER 72—CHOICES MADE

My former high school agriculture teacher, Ralph Kramer, a World War II veteran, was the chairman of the Manitowoc County Draft Board when I received my deferment for the Peace Corps in 1970. After Kenya, I decided to visit him. He had retired from teaching by then. I found him at home. I asked him how he decided to give me a deferment when my draft number was 63. "For one thing, you were fortunate to apply just a few days before Nixon ended those deferments." he said. "Plus, we had plenty of recruits at the time, so we did not need you. But, really, you were not the military type. The Peace Corps was the best place for you." I thanked him for the decision.

Throughout my time in Kenya, I was acutely aware of the sacrifices American soldiers were making in Vietnam. Every time I was bothered by weather, mosquitoes, bad food or corruption, I remembered how safe I was in Kenya, how I did not have to worry about being shot at. At the time, I felt some guilt. Had I not gotten into the Peace Corps, I would have accepted my fate and not tried to stay out of the military. I could imagine driving something like a truck or serving in a support role in Vietnam. The idea of carrying a gun or engaging in violence, however, even in self-defense, was totally against my way of thinking.

In 2011, the Moving Vietnam Wall came for three days to the Veterans' Cemetery in Spooner, Wisconsin, where I live. I was supposed to be in Mali on a project, but a broken ankle kept me at home. I planned to attend some of the festivities. The name of one of my classmates from high school is on the wall, as well as two area neighbors from my hometown in Manitowoc County. I had seen the real Vietnam Veterans Memorial Wall in Washington, D.C. shortly after it opened in the 1980s.

The planning committee needed volunteers to work at the Wall. I was approached by a work colleague in Spooner. He was not a veteran himself but was well-connected to the veteran community. I objected at first, stating that I had not served in the military, much less in Vietnam.

In the end, I agreed to take a six-hour shift on a Sunday afternoon. I could not easily stand at the wall to help people there because I was on crutches, so I sat at one of five computers to help people do a record search on their deceased relative or friend.

I decided to wear a Peace Corps button to see what kind of reaction I would get. The veterans and mourners were magnanimous. I heard many stories of bravery, but more of sorrow about wasted lives. Several people said that, in the Peace Corps, I had at least done something positive for the world. I was even asked to pose with a half-dozen burly motorcycle veterans next to the famous symbol of a lost veteran, the rifle with bayonet in the ground, helmet on top, and boots and tags.

There is still plenty of bitterness. A veteran who survived an ambush in Vietnam said he would never travel anywhere near Vietnam again. In fact, as far as I know, he has not traveled abroad since. A few veterans at other venues told me they were spat on when they returned. One said that both Berkeley and UW-Madison should have had atomic bombs dropped on their campuses. I pondered what a different kind of person I could have become had I been drafted.

I once attended a family reunion of a Peace Corps Paraguay friend. He was a conscientious objector who did alternative service before serving in the Peace Corps. His brother enlisted and served in Vietnam. One of his first cousins fled to Canada. Another first cousin went to prison rather than serve. I did the Peace Corps instead of the military. My wife's ex-husband was also a conscientious objector. It was an interesting reunion!

CHAPTER 73—INFLUENCING

The Peace Corps has three goals for volunteers. They are to teach, to learn, and translate that experience to Americans after returning to the United States. I always felt that my teaching made up about ten percent of the experience and my own learning most of the rest. The more I tried to teach, the more I learned from the experience. I doubt that the third part ever made up more than five percent. With individual exceptions, Americans are occupied with other things. Many are blinded by nationalism. Many lack the foreign exposure to grasp what I was saying. Many, given ignorance or prejudices about things foreign, are disinterested or even hostile to my discoveries.

Two people closer to me who were influenced by my Kenya experience were my first cousin, Kristine Karsteadt, who served in Peace Corps Kenya from 1975-77, and my niece, Sarah Heinemann Schnuelle, who invited me to speak about Kenya to her third-grade classmates in 1989. When I told Sarah later that I was leaving for Ethiopia, she objected. "You cannot leave me now. These are my formative years!"

Living in Kenya for as long as I did, my accent was temporarily altered. I never spoke Kenyan English or picked up much British English; however, my Wisconsin accent became more indistinctly American. I remember coming back to the United States and meeting another American who could not figure out what state or region I was from. He only knew I was not from the South. Then, after about a year in Wisconsin, I met another American on a trip out of state who was listening to me and trying to locate my origins. "You are from somewhere up there, Wisconsin, I think," he said. "Darn!" I told him in jest. "I was hoping to be permanently cured of my Manitowoc-Sheboygan dialect." I did get good at identifying Kenyan English on TV broadcasts.

At the 25th Anniversary Conference of the Peace Corps in Washington D.C. in 1986, I met Peace Corps Volunteer No. 1, Thomas Livingston, who served in Ghana. When he was introduced during the ceremonies, I found myself about three seats away from him. He was quite a modest fellow, not seeking any notoriety. I was also sitting near Mike McCasky, the owner of the Chicago Bears, who had served in some capacity in the Peace Corps. I could not resist introducing myself for what I truly was, a die-hard Packer fan from the Green Bay area. McCasky scowled and then said, "Great team, great opponent!"

I had to admit later that my desire to see the world, help people, and avoid Vietnam were not the only reasons I joined the Peace Corps. I wanted to get out of a culture I found not oppressive, but certainly limiting. Conformity was not a 1960s thing, either.

I recalled my Farmer-to-Farmer extension-training project in northeastern Mozambique in 2011. We were at a meeting in a small, remote Muslim village. At one point in the conversation, a young, likely illiterate woman in the back suddenly raised her hand. "How did you get from there to here?" she asked through the translator. She was not talking about an airplane ride.

I thought for a moment and replied simply, "I left."

I knew at that moment that the young woman who asked me this profound question would probably never leave her village. She would never see what I have seen or experienced. For a fleeting moment, I had the urge to take her hand and yank her out of there. I should have at least hugged her, but her Muslim husband might have objected! Whatever her name, I still remember her.

In 2005, I received the President's Volunteer Service Award for logging an estimated 17,000 volunteer hours, including my six years in the Peace Corps and several international Famer-to-Farmer assignments. The award certificate was signed by President George W. Bush.

Of the 20 Wisconsin agriculture volunteers recruited between 1970-72, I am aware of at least six who later got PhDs. Several did international work. The College of Agriculture and Life Sciences at the University of Wisconsin in Madison gives its highest awards each year to those who have significantly contributed over their careers to the university, the State of Wisconsin, and the greater community. David Wieckert, George Roemer, Bernard Easterday, David Thomas, and I (2016) have received such awards.

CHAPTER 74—EXTERNAL FORCES

W hen I was in graduate school at Ohio University in 1982, we studied different forms of colonialism in Africa. The British tended to employ "separate development" while the French attempted "assimilation" or "association." The German legacy was less pronounced because Germany lost its African colonies after World War I. What was said about Portugal was that it was barely more than a third world country itself, stayed in Africa too long, and had to fight against liberation wars in each of its African colonies. Colonialism forced large changes on Africa, good and bad, and often at a high cost. The reaction to this change depended greatly on the colony involved, the kingdom or tribe involved, and the post-colonial leadership.

I was in Kenya during the Cold War. A few countries in Africa claimed to be non-aligned, like Tanzania, which was really an early friend of the Communist Chinese. Much of the continent was divided up between the West and the Communist Bloc. Kenya was aligned with the British Commonwealth and the West. The Cold War was, in fact, the driver of much of the world politics for the first 40 years of my life.

Despite all the forces, external and internal, that have made and un-made what was supposed to be an ideal Kenya, the people of Kenya have forged a substantial country. Kenya is the economic powerhouse of East Africa. The country welcomes foreign expertise as well as tourism. It is the headquarters of the International Livestock Research Institute (ILRI) with whom I worked in Ethiopia, the International Centre for Research in Agro-Forestry (ICRAF), the United Nations Environment Programme, the United Nations Human Settlements Programme, and many other continental and East African governmental and private organizations.

In 1970, the Peace Corps was still young. Books written about the organization or by former volunteers were rare. For some reason, Ecuador inspired the first three or four books that I read by former volunteers. Ones I remember reading were *The Living Poor* by Moritz Thomsen, *The Making of an Un-American* by Paul Cowan, and *The Barrios of Manta* by Earle and Rhoda Brooks. I spent a night at the Brooks' home in Minnesota in 1975. They owned a large house with ample sleeping space for visitors.

Many volunteers go through a period of questioning the international political and business motives of the United States. I saw how much the United States had its hands in the affairs of foreign countries everywhere, whether it be through big companies, the World Bank, the IMF, commodity extraction, military bases, actual invasions, or just plain interference in the specific country's politics. *Pax americana* (the American version of peace) reigned supreme!

American companies, always claiming to adhere to local foreign regulations, sometimes abandoned their conscience. Around the world, I saw DDT being sold by American companies long after it was banned in the United States. I saw the Marlboro Man on the horse on billboards long after such advertising was banned in the United States.

I did not hate the United States, understanding the inevitable effect of "a big frog in a small pond." I was still proud of what the United States was trying to do, at least in word, to help the world become a better place. My patriotism took on a new form. There was no blind allegiance to the flag, the Constitution, a national religion, a specific race or culture, or the party in power. I saw a flawed superpower that always needed work and updating. I would question anything and everything I was doubtful about. I would, through my Peace Corps experience, become a more respectful, well-rounded, and better-informed citizen, not just of the United States, but of the world.

CHAPTER 75—KWAHERI JACKSON

At the very moment in October of 2016 that I was writing an email to tell Alice Shihundu, Jackson's sister in Nairobi, that I was coming to Kenya in December and planned to see Jackson, she sent an email to inform me that Jackson had died. He died of appendicitis after visiting the doctor twice to complain of abdominal pains. Whatever the level of Kenya medicine at the time, Jackson should not have died from appendicitis.

I sent the following eulogy that was read by Alice at Jackson's funeral: "I am deeply saddened at the passing of Jackson Sikolia Murunga. I would like to express my condolences from my family in America and for all the Peace Corps Volunteers and other Americans who knew and worked with Jackson and may be unaware of his death. Jackson worked for me as an *mpishi* (cook) for almost four years from 1970-74. But he was really my brother. He taught me most of my Swahili and most of what I know about Kenya. Jackson was inevitably right about almost everything, whether it be the character of the people we knew, the culture, or the politics. He was incredibly wise. Jackson had an element of greatness about him that I cannot easily describe. Whenever I had a question or issue about what was going on around me, his counsel was what I inevitably relied on. I am so happy that I was able to return to Kenya several times and that George Roemer and I got to visit and travel around with him in 2013. I was planning to take Jackson around again on my next visit scheduled for December but will be content to visit with the family. Jackson will not be forgotten. I plan to start writing my book about Kenya soon and he will have a big part in it. I plan to meet Jackson in the next life. I will then be his cook and we will continue our many conversations. God Bless!"

I visited Jackson's widows and several of his children at the Lumakanda farm during my project in December to say *kwaheri* (goodbye) to Jackson.

CHAPTER 76—ACKNOWLEDGEMENTS

I would like to thank the people of Kenya, the Government of Kenya, the Peace Corps, the Government of the United States, and the taxpayers of the United States for the wonderful opportunity to serve in the Peace Corps in Kenya.

I would like to thank the late Jackson Sikolia Murunga, his wives Tina and Angela, his siblings and other family members, my housemates George and Sue Roemer, my Kenyan staff and colleagues, and the many Peace Corps volunteers I served with for their assistance, friendship, and inspiration while I served in Kenya. I would like to thank the late David Wieckert for introducing me to Kenya and supporting me throughout my higher education and international career.

I would like to thank the following people for their historical input into this book: Jackson's sister Alice Shihundu; former Peace Corps volunteers George Roemer (Kenya 1970-73) and his wife Sue (private contract teacher in Kenya 1971-73); Alan Johnston (Kenya 1968-71); Peter Petges (Kenya 1969-71); Charles Pike (Kenya 1966-68); Mark Marquardt (Kenya 1970-73); Dennis Syth (Kenya 1970-72); Lee Swan (Kenya 1970-72 program organizer); and Dan Kaiser (civil engineer in Kenya, parts of 1967-74).

I would like to thank the following people for their proofreading of this book: George and Sue Roemer; Alan Johnston; Fern Kanitz (Peace Corps Ecuador 1988-90); my niece Sarah Schnuelle (Wisconsin teacher, reading and writing specialist); and my wife Sherrie Wiegand.

I would further like to thank the Spooner Golf Club for providing me a safe, alternative writing location in their bar and restaurant during the Covid-19 pandemic.

Jackson Sikolia and Otto Wiegand- Former Location
of Otto's House in Tongaren- 2006

CPSIA information can be obtained
at www.ICGtesting.com
Printed in the USA
BVHW090947261021
619746BV00003B/17